ASIA

Cultural Politics in the Global Age

David Birch, Tony Schirato and Sanjay Srivastava

palgrave

ASIA: CULTURAL POLITICS IN THE GLOBAL AGE

First PALGRAVE™ edition: 2001
175 Fifth Avenue, New York, N.Y. 10010 and
Houndmills, Basingstoke, Hampshire, England RG21 6XS
Companies and representatives throughout the world.

PALGRAVE is the new global publishing imprint of St. Martin's Press
LLC Scholarly and Reference Division and Palgrave Publishers Ltd
(formerly Macmillan Press Ltd).

ISBN 0-312-29376-3

A full CIP record for this book is available from the Library of
Congress
A full CIP record for this book is available from the British Library

First paperback edition: 2001
10 9 8 7 6 5 4 3 2 1

Printed and bound in Singapore

Contents

Acknowledgements

For permission to reprint material from works in copyright the authors and publisher make grateful acknowledgement as follows:

The National Health Education Department, Ministry of Health, Singapore

Eagle Flask Industries Limited, Maharashtra, India

Royal Brunei Airlines Sdn.Bhd.

Malaysia Tourism Promotion Board

Ministry of Culture, Arts and Tourism (Australia and New Zealand), Sydney

J.K. Ansell Limited, Mumbai, India

Every effort has been made to trace all the other copyright holders but if any have been inadvertently overlooked the publisher will be pleased to make the necessary acknowledgement at the first opportunity.

Sanjay Srivastava would like to thank the Director and Staff of the International Institute for Asian Studies, Leiden, the Netherlands, where considerable portions of his contribution were written and revised, and thanks also to Radha Khan for help in other ways.

Table and figures

ASIA

Introduction

The region known as Asia has a total population well in excess of three billion people; its peoples speak several hundred different languages and dialects; and it is characterised by a cultural, political, economic and social diversity far greater than anywhere else in the world. Contemporary Asia cannot, by any stretch of the imagination, be considered a homogeneous entity. And yet there is a notion, largely promulgated in the media, that globalisation is reducing the world to a single homogeneous culture.

In fact, globalisation has prompted people worldwide to take more notice of other cultures and aspects of cultural difference, especially with regard to Asia. This can largely be attributed to the rise in power and importance of East Asia, South Asia and Southeast Asia as regional trading and economic blocs (Rowen, 1998). The growth in Asian economic importance in the early 1990s, and the birth of the notion of 'Asian tiger' economies (which referred to Singapore, South Korea, Taiwan and Hong Kong) produced a great deal of 'soul searching' in the west. How could Asia have 'overtaken' traditional economic giants such as the US and the European Union? The answers that came from some parts of Asia itself, particularly Singapore and Malaysia, focused on supposedly 'traditional Asian values' such as a more committed work ethic, the importance of communitarian values (that position the community over the individual), the integration of public and private enterprises, strong central leadership, and a well-resourced education and training sector.

This changed, to a certain extent, with the advent of the so-called 'Asian economic crisis'. The first signs of the crisis can be traced back to early 1997, when a number of South Korean and Thai businesses defaulted on their debts. The so-called 'contagion' quickly spread to other Asian countries such as Indonesia, Malaysia and even Japan. A number of reasons were put forward to explain how and why a group of countries which had, over a period of 30 years, experienced the highest levels of continuous growth in history, should suddenly experience economic collapse. The most prevalent explanations were of the 'bubble effect' variety—Asian economies were overheated; stocks, realty and currencies were overvalued; and most of the affected countries had sizeable current account deficits (in contrast with countries such as Singapore, China and Taiwan, which had considerable surpluses and, to a large extent, avoided 'contamination'). The reason for this 'overheating' could be traced, however, to the integration of those countries into the global economy, firstly as recipients of huge amounts of short-term investment attracted by their growth and high stock and realty values and, secondly, because of the high level of exposure of countries such as Japan to the 'failed' economies (by way of loans, investment, markets). Once businesses defaulted or failed in Thailand and South Korea, international investment was quickly withdrawn, further accentuating the crisis.

Before the crisis many in the West had begun to praise 'Asia's virtues', but now they started to talk about inflexible thinking, nepotism and corruption as 'the Asian way', and the aforementioned virtues became 'traditional Asian vices'. In other words, the various contexts which had given rise to, and stalled, the 'Asian economic miracle' were largely ignored in favour of what were effectively 'racist' stereotypes.

Nevertheless, despite the economic crises of 1997–98 in Southeast Asia which saw many companies fail, thousands of workers laid off and the value of shares and money dramatically reduced afer many years of steady economic growth, many Asian countries have started the twenty-first century with excellent economic prospects, with South Korea and, to a lesser extent, Japan, in particular, leading the way to economic recovery (see Montes & Popov, 1999). But, increasingly, all Asian countries will remain vulnerable to the vagaries and changes of the global economy. Electronic business and commerce, information technology, financial services and tourism, and the knowledge economy, in particular, are likely to become much more important in developing Asian economies as part of a global knowledge economy, particularly in the regional groupings of countries in East Asia, South Asia and Southeast Asia. As such, understanding contemporary Asia against the backdrop of a global economy which, more and more, is governed by the rapid flow of information, is going to become increasingly important, especially in the light of the many political instabilities that still exist—from the internal domestic politics of a Malaysia or Singapore struggling with the idea of accepting serious political opposition, where one-party politics is still very much to the fore, to the growing tensions between Pakistan and India, separated for political reasons when the British pulled out of India in 1947.

This book recognises the importance of understanding contemporary Asia against that global backdrop and, as such, we aim to highlight a number of critical issues which we believe are fundamental in further developing that understanding. We do so for a number of reasons, chief of which is our belief that, in the course of the next few years, the significance of Asia to the global economies of finance, politics and culture will increase. As it increases so, too, will our need to understand contemporary Asia, not just against its histories, which have been well-documented within Asian Studies in universities around the world, but against some of the big picture issues by which we are currently framing our understanding of the modern world, issues like globalisation, technological innovation and transnational flows of information (see Duara, 1995; McGrew & Brook, 1998).

The main economies of Asia (in alphabetical order) are China, Hong Kong (now reunified with China), India, Indonesia, Japan, Malaysia, the Philippines, Singapore, South Korea, Taiwan and Thailand, with Bangladesh, Brunei, Cambodia, Laos, Macau (now reunified with China), Myanmar, Nepal, North Korea, Pakistan, Sri Lanka, Tibet and Vietnam in various stages of economic development.

There is obviously significant diversity and difference among the countries in Asia with respect to their economies and access to information, and in this book we concentrate not so much on the culture-specific details of this diversity, but on some of the underlying (and often connecting) issues and themes that, we believe, will enable culturally literate readings to be made of such diversity. We concentrate on the themes of postcolonialism, globalisation, modernity, postmodernity, and information flows, among others, which, while not specifically unifying the countries of the region (or the world), should enable students and interested readers of the region (both inside and outside) to find a vocabulary for understanding cultural difference and similarity as it impacts upon the cultural politics of modernity in contemporary Asia.

CULTURAL LITERACIES

We use the term 'Asian literacies' to describe our contextualising of Asian cultural politics. The term is derived from the notion of 'cultural literacy', which Schirato and Yell define as 'both a knowledge of meaning systems and an ability to negotiate those systems within different cultural contexts' (Schirato & Yell, 1996/2000: 1). A familiarity with, and understanding of, the 'meaning systems' (policies, contexts, discourses, ideas, ideologies, belief systems, traditions, narratives) that are used (both in the West and within Asia) to represent 'Asia and Asians' helps us to be able to make sense of (or 'negotiate') the ways in which group and individual identities are being created and transformed in contemporary Asia.

This book, then, is about the cultural politics underpinning many of the societies we now call 'Asian', and the need to develop cultural literacies for understanding many aspects of those societies which increasingly, because of globalisation and increased information flows, impact upon the lives of those of us living in different societies.

More than anything else, cultural literacies involve recognising (and being prepared to engage with) cultural difference—not as something to be 'exoticised' and 'othered', as has happened so often in the colonial/neo-colonial histories of many parts of the world, but as discourses of difference which enable us to form opinions, sensibly and sensitively, about the lives, expectations and cultures of other people. These discourses of difference—the many ways in which people express their cultural differences and similarities—form (and inform) the politics of particular cultures.

By 'politics' we mean the ways in which certain types of thinking, acting, perceiving and interpreting are constructed in (and by) different social groups as being important and, in some cases, required, either by law, religious decree, moral standards, social pressures of varying kinds, educational practices and so on, to be practised, accepted and often 'naturalised' as the 'norms' of a society. The fact that a particular 'norm'—for example, prearranged marriages in some social groups, dietary restrictions (like not eating pork or beef) in others—has become accepted as 'normal' involves a cultural politics which has enabled that particular 'norm' to be privileged over and above other possible ways of thinking or being. To understand that underlying cultural politics, we believe, is one of the most effective means of engaging with different cultural literacies.

To be culturally literate, that is, to be able to read the varying discourses of difference without necessarily being expert in a particular culture, requires us to understand at least some of the cultural politics of difference involved in that culture. That requires a critical vocabulary—critical in the sense of being able to stand back and sensibly reflect upon discourses of difference. This book seeks to provide some of that big picture vocabulary through the disciplinary framework of contemporary cultural studies (see Morley & Chen, 1996).

THE POLITICS OF IDENTITY

It is fundamentally important to appreciate that the concept of 'Asia' is not simply a reflection of any 'natural' geographical or cultural entity. Rather, Asia has been 'imagined' into existence within a variety of social, political, economic and cultural contexts. Edward Said's comments about the status of the Orient as an entity are equally applicable to Asia:

> I have begun with the assumption that the Orient is not an inert fact of nature. It is not merely there just as the Occident itself is not just there either. We must take seriously Vico's great observation that men make their own history, that what they can know is what they have made,

and extend it to geography: as both geographical and cultural entities—to say nothing of historical entities—such locales, regions, geographical sectors as 'Orient' and 'Occident' are man-made. Therefore as much as the West itself, the Orient is an idea that has a history and tradition of thought, imagery and vocabulary that has given it reality and presence in and for the West. The two geographical entities thus support and to an extent reflect each other (Said, 1985: 4–5).

The kinds of identity politics that produce notions such as Asia, the Orient and the West impact upon and inform all identities in Asia, regardless of whether they are 'official' (such as the state, or 'legal' political parties) or operate 'unofficially', within or against sanctioned political domains (think of dissident groups in China, or 'religion-based' separatist groups in Indonesia and the Philippines). In other words, communal identities are always based on 'fictions' which try to produce a suspension of disbelief among their members, while also trying to fend off the discontents, inequalities and heterogeneity that they 'gloss over'. Indonesia is a sovereign state: this 'fact' allows Indonesian politicians, bureaucrats, artists, business leaders and military commanders to use the word 'we' to refer to what Benedict Anderson describes as 'many different cultures that have "unified" by political, military, cultural, economic and social processes' (Anderson, 1991: 111). As Anderson points out, to understand what is happening at any time in Indonesia (or any other state in Asia), we need 'to be familiar with the history of how that identity "came about"' (ibid.).

There is a second process, closely related to the construction of this 'we', which is equally important to communal identities and cultural politics in Asia. This involves setting that 'we' against another group or groups who supposedly either don't belong to 'us', and/or threaten 'our' existence. Group identities in Asia, and elsewhere, are always filtered through a politics of 'similarity and difference'. Sometimes this takes the form of politicians and bureaucrats in Asia reproducing orientalist discourses themselves (in a 'positive' way), talking and acting as if states as diverse as Burma, China, India, Indonesia, Pakistan, the Philippines and Vietnam were characterised by some shared 'essence' ('traditional Asian values' such as communitarian values) as opposed to the 'vices of the west' (individualism, decadence, sexual depravity and laziness are the 'usual suspects' here).

In an age of global culture, transnational capitalism and communication technologies that are threatening to erase the differences of time and place, there is a danger that the convergence between global and local contexts that informs identity politics in Asia will be subsumed, in the West, into a general, oversimplified and inaccurate, view of Asia; what has been called 'the Asian view' (see Preston, 1998). At the same time, 'new' ideas of Asia are being constructed by those in Asia who were once colonised, and who now seek to define modernity in their societies in 'Asian' rather than in 'European' (or American) ways. How these societies determine the ways in which the social, political, economic and cultural identities of their communities are constructed is crucial to understanding cultural politics in contemporary Asia (see Lowe & Lloyd, 1997). This book will not enable you to become a cultural expert with regard to specific Asian societies or traditions, but it will help you develop a cultural literacy with regard to the major themes, issues and contexts that characterise the cultural politics of 'contemporary Asia'.

SUGGESTIONS FOR FURTHER READING

Lowe, Lisa and David Lloyd (eds) (1997) *The Politics of Culture in the Shadow of Capital*, in the series *Post-Contemporary Interventions*, general editors Stanley Fish and Frederic Jameson, Duke University Press, Durham and London

Montes, Manuel F. and Vladimir V. Popov (1999) *The Asian Crisis Turns Global*, Institute of Southeast Asian Studies, Singapore

Preston, Peter (1998) *Pacific Asia in the Global System: An Introduction*, Blackwell, Oxford

Schirato, Tony and Susan Yell (1996) *Communication and Cultural Literacy: An Introduction*, 2nd edn 2000, Allen & Unwin, Sydney; published as *Communication and Culture* by Sage, London

1

The idea of Asia

Many politicians, bureaucrats, journalists, business people
(and academics) write and talk about Asia as if there was a
physical or cultural reality that corresponds to that term. In a
sense, however, there is no such thing as 'Asia', any more than
there is a physical reality behind the notion of 'the West'.
'Asia', like 'the West', is a geographical, cultural and political
idea, but an idea which people, both in Asian countries and
throughout the world, think of as a reality. Some western
politicians and economists have talked about the 'Asian
economic miracle' of the past few decades, and more recently
about the 'Asian economic crisis', as if there was a single, homogeneous entity—'Asia'—which the West either was competing
against and had to copy (pre-crisis), or could feel (once again)
comfortably superior towards (post-crisis).

The pre-crisis mentality often represented Asia—in both
western and Asian media, as well as in other cultural texts—
as being populated by extraordinarily zealous and
hard-working populations, as much machines as human
beings, underselling and outperforming (and as a consequence, making redundant) western labour. The post-crisis
mentality, on the other hand, has tended to represent Asia
in most media as a place supposedly characterised by
endemic corruption and cronyism, negative activities which
have seriously undermined the 'positive' western legacies of
democracy and a market-driven economy 'given' to Asia
through the processes of colonisation.

The idea of Asia has also been promulgated through the knowledge-gathering practices of academic life. 'Area Studies', an important aspect of liberal arts education in North America (and one that has also had historical linkages with the United States defence forces), has strongly influenced representations and understandings of Asia. By defining the characteristics seen as capturing the 'essence' of different Asian civilisations, Area Studies was instrumental in setting in place rigid frameworks of analysis which are increasingly challenged in contemporary Asian Studies today; the centrality of the village, filial piety and hierarchy in definitions of the 'real Asia' owe much to the particular academic (and political) ways of constructing Asia.

The image of the western colonising nation is a powerful and important one for understanding contemporary Asia, because while there may well have been physical invasion and colonial appropriation (in contemporary Indonesia, Malaysia, Singapore, Hong Kong, Macau, Myanmar, the Philippines, India, Pakistan and Vietnam), often a more insidious 'colonising attitude' has naturalised the idea of European/American superiority, and exoticised and orientalised the non-European/ American people of the world (see Harlow & Carter, 1999).

Western stereotypes of Asia and Asians have existed for hundreds of years, and they continue to exert a strong influence on the way peoples and countries in Asia are represented, understood and treated. What we will do in this book is to describe some of these stereotypes, and consider how, and for what reasons, they continue to be produced. In order to begin this, we will look in detail, and give examples of, what Edward Said has identified as the processes, attitudes and discourses of 'orientalism'.

Said's book *Orientalism*, which was first published in 1978, puts forward the argument that the many different kinds of representations (books, policy documents, films, operas, television shows, media reports) of the Orient by the West are tied in with colonialist politics. In other words, there is no essential distinction between supposedly 'neutral' and apolitical cultural texts which deal with Asia and Asians (say, a Puccini opera, Rudyard Kipling's book *Kim*, or a Hollywood film such as *The King and I*), and obvious anti-Asian political practices (the western invasion of China and other Asian countries in the nineteenth century, or racist, anti-Asian politics in contemporary Australia, Britain, Canada, New Zealand and the US).

Said bases this idea on four related arguments about the West's representations and understanding of the Orient. The first of these is that 'orientals' are 'other than human', with 'true' or 'full' humanness being associated with the West. This was very much a position associated with the early days of colonialism, when, for example, the Chinese were not allowed into certain parts of colonised Shanghai; or notices would appear on theatres, as was the case with the Victoria Theatre in Singapore, announcing that neither dogs nor Chinese were allowed inside.

The second is that these representations—produced by scientists, academics, school teachers, politicians, business people, journalists, novelists and film makers—have come to constitute a body of knowledge that enables the West to understand 'the truth' about the 'Orient' and 'orientals'. The third is that these cultural and political explanations have been the basis for the West taking a superior position—intellectually, morally, ethically, politically—with regard to the 'Orient' and 'orientals'. Fourthly, in the process this 'superiority mentality' has justified western intervention in Asian countries' affairs, ranging from sending gunboats into China in the nineteenth century, to the International Monetary Fund dictating financial, social and political policies during the 'Asian economic crisis'.

These attitudes remain today in many places, both within and outside of contemporary Asia, despite the fact that Asia is no longer a colonised region. There is often an internal colonial attitude left behind, long after the departure of the colonisers—what is called by some commentators 'endo-colonialism', despite the fact that many of the countries concerned may now be described as postcolonial.

There is also, often, a lingering view that, despite having physically left a country, a colonising nation retains a perspective on that country which is still determined by colonialist attitudes—what is often called neo-colonialism. We are interested, in this book, in all of these: colonialism, endo-colonialism, neo-colonialism and postcolonialism, and the 'orientalist' perceptions and attitudes that have generally gone (and often still go) hand in hand with them. Recognising and understanding these attitudes is an essential means of developing a cultural literacy in being able to sensitively read contemporary Asia and its reactions to modernity/postmodernity (see Ashcroft et al., 1998). Many of these orientalist attitudes and perceptions may still lie at the heart of many discourses and texts (print media, film, radio, television, Internet, advertising and so on) which present the many images of contemporary Asia both inside and outside of Asia. These discourses and texts form the core of our understanding of other cultures.

A political practice, like an invasion, can be read as a text just as a newspaper article can be, and there may well be orientalist attitudes to be read in both (see Spivak, 1987). The idea of a practice, or activity, functioning in much the same way as a written text, or a film, or a performance on stage, is one which lies at the very heart of contemporary cultural studies, and one which is central to the way we present the ideas, issues and material in this book. It is for that reason, for example, that we argue here that the concept of Asia is based not so much on the reality of Asia as Asia—pre-existing the politics, cultures and social lives that now are identified with being Asian—but on the imagining of Asia as a text, an idea, a cultural construction, imagined as Asia rather than existing 'naturally' as Asia. The notion of 'orientalism', therefore, is a cultural construction, expressed through discourses and texts that vary from the print media to the political practices of invasion. It has been a major theme in the construction of Asia by the West, and also in the resistance to (and sometimes the acceptance of) this western construction by those who have been labelled by the West (and by themselves, with the notable exception of the Japanese) as 'Asians' (see Tanaka, 1993).

CULTURAL IDENTITIES

A group or community is always constructed, to some extent, in terms of what it is different from, or opposed to (see Clifford, 1988). If you were to ask Croatians or Bosnians about their identity, part of their response might be about 'not being Yugoslavs'. Much the same process is true of many Kashmiri Muslims in India, and of sections of the Tamil population of Sri Lanka: their identities are based on 'identifying against' other groups. In fact in all of these examples, 'not being the other' is perhaps the most significant factor in establishing and maintaining group identity. Some Croatians, Bosnians, Kashmiri Muslims and Tamils might constitute themselves as a group by saying that they are not devious, barbaric and inhuman—which is what they claim their 'others' are.

The 'Orient' has long played the part of western 'other', particularly in times of crisis: the Turks for sixteenth-century Europe; Japan during the Second World War, and to a certain extent during the decline of western economic dominance over the last 20 years; and China during the nineteenth-century gold rushes in America and Australia, and the Korean War (see Williams & Chrisman, 1994). 'Orientals', repeatedly characterised by some western texts as alternatively lazy, stupid, mindless, barbaric and untrustworthy, have served as a guarantee of the 'superiority' of the Briton, American, German or Australian over many years (see Lowe, 1991). European immigrants, for example, recently arrived on the goldfields of Australia in the late nineteenth century, would caution their friends not to look directly into the eyes of a 'Chinaman', otherwise desperate bad luck would follow, and yet in the years to come it was these very 'Chinamen' who would provide the bulk of the fresh vegetables that the thriving goldfields towns would eat.

Edward Said argues that in orientalist texts western identity is marked out as different from that of orientals in terms of their political organisations (parliament, democracy), science and technology, legal systems, religion, clothes and eating habits—that is to say, in terms of their culture. Markers of cultural difference are assigned a specific value: being a Christian is read, in the West, as making a person thoughtful, pious and sensitive, while Muslims are often represented as fanatical, violent, irrational and cruel. In other words, possessing an 'inferior culture' is one of the rationales which 'justifies' people being treated as less than human, and, of course, many were, and still are treated that way around the world.

The production of the binary 'West/Orient' has been naturalised in much of western culture, and this has largely determined how the West has understood and reacted to Asia and Asians (see Turner, 1994). Of course, 'orientalist' representations of Asia have not remained the same. The kinds of things that could be said and written about Asia in the colonial era (say, before many Asian states fought hard for their independence) differed considerably from how the West represented peoples and countries (for instance, Japan) that were now, in economic terms, equally powerful and prosperous. Cultural texts have produced 'orientalist' versions of Asia and its peoples for many years.

Gunga Din (1939), for example, is a classic Hollywood film about three British soldiers who, with some timely help from a subservient Indian, overcome a rebellion that threatens British control of India. A later film, *Blood Oath* (1988), is set at the end of the Second World War, and is concerned with the attempts of an Australian army officer to bring to justice Japanese soldiers who allegedly committed war crimes. *Gunga Din* was produced when the British Empire, and western colonialism, were still a dominant force in Asia. *Blood Oath*, on the other hand, was released at a time when this geo-political context was an object of nostalgic reflection.

Orientalist representations are at work in both films. Even before *Gunga Din* starts, a dark, 'exotic' Indian strikes a huge gong. The Indian is a slave serving a colonial master—the British Raj. The title character in the film is equally subservient and unimposing. He is short, weakly built, and tends to break into exaggerated, childlike smiles whenever the British appear. Gunga Din is in no way physically powerful or potentially threatening. The three British soldiers, on the other hand, are not only strong and good fighters, but regularly subdue, beat up and dispose of 'natives' (throwing them around in a 'comical' manner).

There is no way, given the codes of physicality operating in the film, that the character of Gunga Din can be taken seriously, be treated as an equal of the heroes, or be in control of his destiny. He is, in every way, an Indian child in a world of British adults.

In this context, the figure of Gunga Din is also a counter to that of the Anglicised and 'disloyal' educated Indian who, during the latter phase of colonialism, was seen to be in the vanguard of movements demanding greater rights for native subjects. These latter were the objects of great scorn by the British for their 'mimicry' of western ways (including the demands for greater political rights and freedom). Gunga Din may not have had much formal education, but he was, nevertheless, noble and 'manly' because, unlike groups such as the 'effeminate Bengali' (Sinha 1997), he was true to himself through his recognition of his 'station in life'.

Indeed, as part of this perspective, there had developed a discourse of differences between 'martial' and 'non-martial' races (Omissi 1991), the former being far preferable in British eyes for their lack of 'pretensions' to be the equal of their colonial masters. In our time, the colonial discourse on 'martial races' continues to flourish in western representations of the Gurkhas of Nepal, masking in turn their economic marginality which is an important factor in their seeking a military career.

Sixty years later it would be almost impossible to produce a film like *Gunga Din*. The end of overt colonialism in Asia and elsewhere, and the increase in the economic and political power of Asian countries has produced geo-political contexts which make it harder to justify the subservience of Asia to the West. But as the 1988 film *Blood Oath* demonstrates, there is a marked transition from colonial to contemporary orientalism. In *Blood Oath* the Japanese are, like the Thugs in *Gunga Din*, the perpetrators of sadistic, mindless violence. And, again like the Thugs, they can think and act only as a group, not as individuals. This Australian film makes it clear, however, that given access to the right civilising influences (Christianity, western democracy), the Japanese could become civilised, rational, free-thinking westerners. Whereas in *Gunga Din* the idea of Indians becoming 'civilised' was a pretence, in *Blood Oath* there is a sense that the Japanese can really be 'de-orientalised'.

The film's representation of the Japanese as 'sadistic orientals' takes place, firstly, through scenes of mass graves, brutal beatings and executions; and secondly, in terms of their callous responses when, on trial for war crimes, they are confronted with evidence of what they have done. The film spends a lot of time showing exhumations and mass beatings, but what is presented in the film as even more shocking and inhuman is the refusal of the Japanese to feel or demonstrate any remorse. Vice-Admiral Takahashi, the officer in charge at the time, is a hypocritical liar unwilling to admit his complicity, while Ikeuchi, the officer in charge of daily affairs, laughs openly in court when another soldier 'confesses'. The examples of their lack of remorse and conscience are many and varied: they respond to questions mechanically, their faces remain impassive when details of the atrocities are given (until Ikeuchi finally laughs and gives himself away), and in the middle of the trial they both exhibit a commitment to their 'national code' (supposedly based on rigid discipline, honour and ruthlessness), which presumably produced the war crimes in the first place.

The Australian officer who prosecutes the Japanese—the self-righteous, and often violent, hero of the film—understands what is happening with Takahashi's performance of being westernised. He argues that by allowing Takahashi to get off unpunished, and in attempting to use him in the 'reconstruction' of Japan, the Americans are ensuring that Japanese culture won't change. Change will only come, he argues, when those 'at the top' (the news of the pardoning of the Emperor Hirohito is referred to by the Australians, with incredulity, during the film) are 'humiliated', and removed from office.

The interesting thing about the change in orientalist representations from *Gunga Din* to *Blood Oath* is that whereas in the earlier film the superiority of the West over the Asian could be backed up by evidence of western technical, military and economic dominance, *Blood Oath* has to argue for western superiority without any such 'hard proof'. The loss of western dominance in these areas can be put down to 'devious oriental trickery'. While the West played by 'civilised rules', and thought that the war was over, Japan 'performed' western civilisation in order to atone for its military defeat—economics in this case being war by other means. The West, as far as *Blood Oath* is concerned, is still 'morally superior', even as it loses out on the economic front.

We could say that these examples are only 'fictions' and entertainment, and that they don't really reflect everyday attitudes, or political and social realities. But Said's point is that these kinds of 'orientalist' stories, which perpetuate stereo-types about Asia and Asians, are accepted as 'the truth' by many people, whether they are politicians, business people, journalists or people responding to opinion polls about 'dangerous levels of Asian immigration'. And there are very real consequences of those beliefs—in the decisions politicians and business people make, in the way journalists report stories about Asian countries and in the way people treat Asian migrants.

ORIENTALISM AND THE MEDIA

There are many examples in contemporary political, economic and ordinary social life of 'orientalism' in action. The problems that struck the Indonesian, South Korean and Thai economies in 1997–98, for example, were interpreted by politicians, world economic organisations and business journalists as resulting from supposedly endemic 'Asian vices' such as cronyism and corruption. This interpretation is (often unwittingly) based on the racist assumption, central to both *Gunga Din* and *Blood Oath*, that westerners are more honest, and socially and politically more 'mature', than Asians.

Echoes of this can be found in the negative media coverage (particularly in Australia) of charges of 'match-fixing' against certain Pakistani cricketers, and of 'unsporting' behaviour against the Sri Lankan team captain Arjuna Ranatunga, while considerably more sympathetic treatment seems to have been given to Hansie Cronje, the white South African cricket captain who would later confess to taking bribes from Indian bookmakers. While the subsequent involvement of certain Australian cricketers in illegal betting in India was dismissed as inconsequential and resulting from naivety, the actions of the Pakistanis came to stand for the supposed corruption of subcontinental life in general. And Ranatunga, who publicly questioned Australian umpires over their disregard for the rulings of the international cricket administrative body, was immediately vilified as the oriental who had no regard for the 'rules' of the game and sought to win through 'underhanded' means.

The underlying (but usually unstated) argument is that the West is more reasonable and rational, and more 'human', because of its supposed long tradition of respect for democracy, justice and public accountability. This attitude translates into a position where organisations such as the World Bank and the International Monetary Fund feel that they need to force Asian governments and nations to 'take their medicine', which usually means giving up sovereignty over their own economic and social affairs and policies.

The analogy at work here is that the West is the parent, and Asia is the child, a position which provided the rationale for colonialist policies in the nineteenth and early twentieth centuries, and which was used by the British, French and

Dutch governments in opposing independence movements in countries such as India, Vietnam and Indonesia. It still turns up, not just in the kinds of political and economic discourses that justify western intervention in Asian affairs, but often in the western media's reporting of contemporary Asian events.

A good example of this was the reporting of events in Indonesia following the 'economic crisis' of 1997–98. The numerous outbreaks of violence (in Timor, Aceh, Sumatra and Java) were largely brought about by two major factors. First among these was Indonesia's experience of the Asian economic crisis, which was provoked by western investors speculating against, and selling down, the local currency (the rupiah). This resulted in the International Monetary Fund intervening in Indonesian affairs, forcing the government to cut spending. There were a number of very severe, and immediate, social consequences: people lost their jobs, the currency lost its value, businesses closed down, and the price of food and other necessities rose dramatically, causing widespread hardship and, in many cases, starvation. Secondly, the Soeharto government's violent repression of political opponents (students, Islamic groups, pro-democracy reformers, intellectuals) and separatist movements (in places such as East Timor, Ambon and Aceh) fermented discontent. The combination of the two factors set off a chain reaction of looting, riots, pogroms and 'mini wars'.

There is an interesting parallel here between contemporary media representations of riots in Indonesia and portrayals of 'disorder' in the colonial era. In his analysis of nineteenth-century British records dealing with Hindu–Muslim conflicts in India, the historian Gyanendra Pandey, for example, speaks of the emergence of the 'communal riot narrative' (Pandey 1994: 62). Irrespective of the reasons for and extent of such conflicts, the British, Pandey notes, appeared to employ an unvarying explanatory framework, and within this narrative all such riots became 'simply the reflexive actions of an irrational people' (Pandey 1994: 62) who were prone to 'fanaticism' and 'mindless' violence.

The western media's coverage of these events was virtually free of any identification or analysis of the causes of the violence, or of the West's role in provoking and facilitating it. Although there were general references to economic hardship and political dissent, these were usually couched in simplistic terms which fitted in with orientalist stereotypes of Asia. For instance, the 'food riots' in Indonesia in 1998–99 were generally reported as if they were, in a sense, 'natural' and inevitable. The riots were contextualised by presenting Indonesia, like most Asian countries, as endemically poor, backward, overcrowded—and pretty much without hope. The resulting violence could be understood, then, as arising out of the ignorance, poverty, misery and hopelessness of life in Indonesia. In a sense the food riots served, for the western media, as both cause and effect regarding Indonesia's problems: they demonstrated an 'oriental' tendency towards irrationality and barbarism, which was preventing Indonesia ever progressing towards western levels of development, and which condemned its people to an endlessly repeating cycle of poverty and violence.

Stories and reports concerning the various independence movements were contextualised within the same orientalist logic. The situation in East Timor was represented, quite simply, as an attempt by one group of people (the East Timorese) to throw off the yoke of a corrupt and despotic Asian regime. What these reports ignored, of course, was that the East Timorese had originally been colonised by one western nation (Portugal), and had then been virtually 'handed over' to Indonesian control through the compliance, and perhaps even at the urging, of another (Australia).

The western media's reporting of events in Indonesia in 1998–99 demonstrated how orientalist discourses, attitudes, values and logics still inform the West's understanding and representations of Asia and Asians. Much the same happens, however, when the western media reports on Asian communities in western countries.

In March 1998, for example, Australian television news covered a story about the search for the killer of a Sydney politician who was campaigning against the drug trade in his electorate, centred on the suburb of Cabramatta. In the 1980s a large number of Vietnamese migrants arrived in Australia and, according to some media reports, virtually 'took over' the place. The most obvious example of the difference between Cabramatta and other communities—at least as far as the media were concerned—was that drug trafficking was going on unchecked there. Of couse, drug trafficking was probably going on, largely unchecked, in many Sydney suburbs. But Cabramatta caught the media's attention because of its Vietnamese population, and its 'highly visible' Asian culture (shops, temples, restaurants). When a local (white) politician was murdered, the media produced special reports; long interviews with 'embattled' police, and documentaries dealing with this new and threatening phenomenon—the consequences of the 'Asianising' of (a part of) Australia (see Milner & Quilty, 1996; Fitzgerald, 1997). At the same time the government attempted to exploit what it presumed to be widespread 'anti-Asian' sentiment by cutting back on levels of Asian immigration, while a new political party called One Nation, headed by Pauline Hanson, achieved considerable electoral success campaigning on what was virtually a return to a 'White Australia' policy.

The western media's reporting of these, and many other, stories involving Asia and Asians is based on, or strongly shaped by, the discourses and attitudes which Said identified and described as orientalism. The examples we have examined, so far, represent or understand Asia as lacking humanity, civilisation and a sense of individuality. Media reports of violence in Indonesia in 1997–99, for example, represent and describe 'the people' as rampaging mindlessly around the streets, without purpose or hope. And the media's coverage of events in Cabramatta consistently emphasised how the establishment of an 'Asian community' in Australia had resulted in the breakdown of 'law and order'. In both cases what defines Asians is their 'lack of humanity'—mass slaughter, pillaging, drug dealing and other criminal activities demonstrate a barbarism not yet uplifted by 'civilisation', one of the principal reasons why the images of the evidence of the slaughter of so many East Timorese by the pro-Indonesia militia, and the Indonesian army itself, stirred up so much concern around the world and sent the Australians in to restore 'order'. 'Whose order?' was the question raised in many countries in Asia, as the image of the 'white man' riding in to save the people from Asian barbarity flashed around the world.

The old colonial markers of civilisation, such as respect for the (western) law, are invoked, often indirectly, as explanations of the 'inhumanity' occurring in Indonesia, East Timor or Cabramatta. But one of the most important points that Said makes about orientalist discourses is that they are flexible: any aspect of oriental culture can be produced as a sign of inhumanity and barbarism (see Bhabha, 1990, 1994). Contemporary orientalist representations of economically 'successful' countries such as Japan and Singapore, for instance, cannot be based on their disregard for the law, or their lack of science and technology, education, capitalism or democracy. Here the *Blood Oath* model of orientalism is more relevant. Japan and Singapore 'appear' to have embraced western civilisation (democracy, market economy, respect for human rights), but this is often more of an illusion than reality.

We made the point at the beginning of this chapter that Asia, like 'the West', is an idea—but one which can be used, at different times and in different ways, for political purposes. In the colonial period the enslavement of millions of people was perpetuated, maintained and justified through reference to orientalist notions that Asians were 'like children', and it was the West's duty—the so-called 'white man's burden'—to civilise them, and bring them into 'adulthood'. This attitude still informs much of the West's dealing with Asia, but the 'direct intervention' and blatant racism of nineteenth-century colonialism have largely been replaced by the 'paternalism' of bodies such as the World Bank and the International Monetary Fund.

These stereotypes of Asia and Asians that circulate in contemporary western cultures aren't the same as those that cropped up in, say, nineteenth-century England, nor are they necessarily consistent from one context to another. Orientalist logic can be used to characterise the Japanese as clever, hard-working, single-minded and ruthless, and consequently as a threat to jobs and living standards in the West. Or it can represent Indonesians as lazy, ignorant, corrupt, irrational and more or less deserving of any trouble or violence that befalls them. What is consistent about orientalism, and its earlier deployment in colonial contexts, is that it naturalises not just peoples ('Asians aren't really fully human'), but power relations ('Asia is inferior, and should be subordinate, to the West'). These discourses, attitudes and narratives have characterised, and continue to inform, much of the West's relationship with, and representations of, Asia and Asians (see Kabbani, 1986).

IMAGINING ASIA

The use of racial and national stereotypes, or the promotion of values and traditions as the basis of cultural superiority, is not confined to the West's relations with Asia. One of the most prominent aspects of contemporary Asian cultural politics is the debate about, and the strong state endorsement of, the notion of 'Asian values' (see Birch, 1998). There are three main contexts driving this process. The first is the ongoing process of states seeking to bind together disparate classes, ethnicities and religious groups in order to maintain the 'imagined community' that is the nation. This has always been a precarious business, and not just in Asia. National identities, if they are to be perpetuated, continually need to be 're-imagined', and the ideals and values on which they are based brought 'up to date', in order to appease or counter the many 'discontents' that threaten them.

The second context is the playing out of the relationship, in postcolonial Asia, between nationalism and the imperatives of modernisation. The two are normally thought to go hand in hand, but insofar as the processes of modernisation are often linked to old colonial institutions, discourses, values and practices, there is always a potential tension between them.

An important aspect of this is the manner in which the seeming contradictions between 'modernity' and 'tradition' have been negotiated through the framework of nationalism. In fact, it may be more useful to argue that postcolonial experience shows that the contradictions are more apparent than real. For, as we will show, nationalist discourses in Asia have been an important site for the 'modernisation of traditions', such that nationalists have argued that while there may exist 'traditions' which may be inimical to the aims of modernity, these in fact belong to 'irrational' populations—such as women and Aboriginal populations—in their midst, and that Asian societies also possess 'rational' traditions that can be recuperated for the purposes of creating 'modern' nation-states.

The third context, closely linked to the first two, is tied up with the processes of neo-colonialism and globalisation. Developments in contemporary communication technology (videos, faxes, satellite and cable television, the Internet) are diminishing a state's ability to monitor and regulate the information and cultural texts that flow across and within its physical boundaries. Equally importantly, a state's economic 'well-being' is now largely at the mercy of multinational and transnational corporations, and the 'whims' of the global marketplace. The inability of the state to control its own cultural or economic destiny constitutes a potentially fatal threat to national sovereignty in Asia and elsewhere.

It is useful to look at these three contexts in more detail. National identity is largely about the state and its various ideological apparatuses (the media, schools, bureaucracies) producing a public consciousness of 'eternal and unquestionable values' that bind people together, and which differentiate 'us' (the nation which shares these values) from 'them' (those who threaten those values from both inside and out). Given the political, economic and social pressures that are working to clearly differentiate many groups living within national boundaries in Asia (the anti-Chinese pogroms in Indonesia are one example), there is a need, on the part of the state, for one 'overriding' set of values to nullify 'nationalist discontents'—which is where the promotion of 'Asian values' comes in.

The lead in this area was taken by President Sukarno's Indonesia after it gained independence from the Dutch. It developed *Pancasila*, a state ideology gradually put in place during the last 50 years, as a way of unifying—actually, creating—something called Indonesia. The main components of *Pancasila* are a belief in one God, humanitarianism, national unity, democracy through consensus and social justice. The ideas contained in *Pancasila*—or at least the way they were interpreted—dominated Indonesian public and private life. Every student and citizen had to take a compulsory course in understanding them, and people's actions and utterances were measured against them.

Pancasila was developed as a means of unifying very diverse cultures into a single nation. At independence a number of choices faced the Preparatory Assembly for Indonesian Independence, such as whether independent Indonesia should become a secular nationalistic state, or whether Islam should become its ideological basis. President Sukarno initially proposed five core principles which were incorporated, with revisions and changes being made over the years, into the Indonesian Constitution. The idea was to establish a set of principles which were deeply rooted in the traditional values of the many different 'Indonesian' cultures, and which would get their relevance from the fact that *Pancasila* means the fundamental consensus on which the willingness to join the common Indonesian state is based.

In a sense, however, *Pancasila* doesn't, and couldn't, exist. Why? Because if there really was a set of core values that could be readily identified, they would invariably be more exclusive than inclusive. Diverse ethnic groups and cultures aren't likely to agree on 'core values'—there would always be some part of those values that was antithetical to a group's identity or beliefs. The idea of gender equality, for instance, might seem unproblematical, but it could be read by some Muslims as anti-Islamic.

Pancasila functioned, then, not as a set of 'positives' that could be identified and agreed upon, but as an 'empty' set of terms which could be 'filled in' at any time by different groups in accordance with their own traditional values. But *Pancasila* could also be used as a political weapon: whoever was in a position to decide what it 'really' meant could effectively accuse opponents of being anti-Indonesian. *Pancasila* actually came about precisely for this purpose; it was put up, to some extent, as a bulwark against the idea of an 'Islamic Indonesia'. More recently it has been used to denounce both Islamic political aspirations, and independence movements in East Timor, Ambon and Aceh.

ASIAN NATIONALISM AND MODERNISATION

The second context in which the idea of Asian values has figured prominently is in terms of the often mutually exclusive imperatives associated with nationalism and modernisation. Modernisation is usually understood as being about progress, about change, and breaking free from outdated traditions. And yet as we pointed out earlier, states invariably use supposed 'ancient' traditions, beliefs and values as the glue with which to bind different groups together as a nation. We also suggested that nationalist discourses attempt a reconciliation between 'modernity' and 'tradition' through the 'modernisation of traditions'. Certain customs and traditions are presented as being capable of bearing the 'load' of modernity, while at the same time adding a 'national' (or indigenous) flavour to it.

Indeed, this would appear to be an important principle of differentiation operating within non-western discourses of modernity, one which suggests that Asians may become modern, without having to become westernised, and that the maintenance of selected local traditions are fundamental to this objective. Let us consider some examples.

An important context often invoked by the colonial rulers in India to illustrate the 'inferiority' of 'native' lifestyles was the supposedly debilitating effects of Hinduism upon all efforts to 'modernise' indigenous existence. Hinduism advocated beliefs and actions, it was asserted, that led to, among other things, passivity, 'other-worldliness', and a fatalistic attitude that was contrary to 'progress'. Indian nationalist thinking reacted to this through suggesting that *that* kind of Hinduism was only practised by 'backward' people and that, in fact, certain other traditions were in concord with western thinking on the matter. So, the philosopher-president S. Radhakrishnan (1888–1975) suggested that though there existed a body of 'crude beliefs' within Hinduism, *educated* Indians did not subscribe to them and, in time, such crudities would be 'eradicated' by 'civilisation' (Srivastava 1998). In addition, he noted, the Hindu view on the superiority of certain groups in society, as expressed through the caste system, was compatible with ancient Greek thinking (and hence modern western thought) on heredity and 'racial' superiority. Here, nationalist arguments, including the Gandhian, suggested that caste was an 'essential element of Indian society' (Chatterjee 1993: 174) and denied 'the charge that caste is necessarily contradictory to, and incompatible with, a modern and just society' (ibid.). India could be both 'modern' and remain 'Indian'.

Our second example of recuperation of tradition for the purposes of modernity is also drawn from the work of President Radhakrishnan. The principle of the free market was an important cornerstone of early theorising on capitalism by economists such as Alfred Marshall. Colonised societies, it came to be argued, could not sustain rapid development and modernisation, characterised as they were by an absence of conditions that made for a free market. Nationalists such as Radhakrishnan had an answer to this as well. Echoing the refrain of the *laissez-faire* theorists, he noted that the holy text *Bhagvadgita* taught that 'the world is so arranged that each man's good turns out to be the good of others' (Radhakrishnan quoted in Srivastava 1998: 62).

Once again, modernity without westernisation. Leela Gandhi, referring to the work of Tom Nairn, explains it this way:

> It is Nairn's contention that the genetic code of all national-ism is simultaneously inscribed by the contradictory signals of what he calls 'health' and 'morbidity': 'forms of "irration-ality" ' (prejudice, sentimentality, collective egoism, aggres-sion etc.) stain the lot of them. If the rhetoric of national development secures a forward-looking vision, the corres-ponding—and equally powerful—rhetoric of national attachment invokes the latent energies of custom and tradi-tion (1998: 106).

This combination of modernity and tradition is at the heart of attempts by some leaders in Asia to promote 'authentic' Asian ways of defining modernity and national identity. Those terms have increasingly involved a synthesising of 'Asian' tradi-tion and 'western' technologies.

The fit between the two has not always been comfortable, especially in the area of western-driven information and media flows which are often considered to be damaging to specific 'Asian' cultural values. This has led to a romanticising of 'older', more traditional Asian ways, as the basis of a distinctive 'Asian modernity'. Consider, for example, the advertisement for Royal Brunei Airlines in Figure 1 (similar, in many ways to advertise-ments for Singapore International Airlines, Cathay Pacific and Thai Airways) which paints an idealised image of modern tech-nology as a form of traditional 'Asian' crafts.

This presents Asia as a tapestry—a weave of old and new, tradition and innovation, East and West, local and global, but with a very specific foregrounding of the concept of 'Asia' and 'Asian'. Asia here is part of a global picture, but not because it has simply borrowed modernity from the 'west'. It has built upon values, the message makes clear, which predate the 'West' but, above all, are 'Asian'. The point here is to showcase not just an airline, but an airline which is synonymous both with Brunei, 'Asia' and 'immortal' Asian values.

This is a very common way of presenting the 'credentials' for a company operating in Asia. Consider, for example, Figure 2 on page 20, which shows an advertisement, for a leading Japanese company, Mitsui.

Figure 1   Royal Brunei Airlines advertisement, 1998

Picking up on the theme of the fires that engulfed much of Southeast Asia for many months in 1997, this advertisement emphasises the idea of Asia as a distinct 'place' and 'entity' in which a *Sogo Shosha* (meaning an international trading company) can operate as 'Asian'. There is an international corporate identity established here which seeks to define itself in terms of a regional 'Asian' identity, developing the theme that Asia can be understood in terms of both its 'ancient cultures' and its 'promise for tomorrow'. This idea of a cultural fusion is a dominant one across Asia, but the cultural politics operating here, in particular, seeks to establish a position which sees a 'new Asia' as the power broker in international affairs. In other words, it is Asia which is forging a new world because of its combination of tradition and technology.

What makes this process particularly complex, however, is that the attempt by some governments in Asia to partake of the (predominantly economic) benefits associated with modernity and postmodernity is only a partial commitment. Modernisation, at least theoretically, is not just about technology, science, education and higher living standards. It is often equated with values such as individuality, respect for human rights, democracy, certain legal codes and practices, and

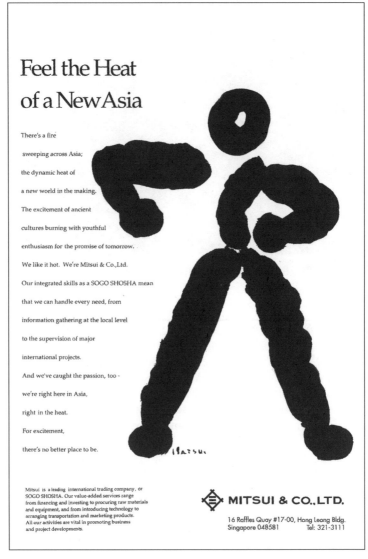

Figure 2   Mitsui & Co. Ltd advertisement, 1998

freedom of speech. However, as with *Pancasila*, because these terms are flexible in meaning, different groups fight over them, and try to use them to their own advantage (see Laothamatas, 1997). During the Indonesian invasion of East

Timor, for instance, local independence groups appealed to the West (mainly the US) for help on the basis that they were being denied their democratic and human rights—values to which the West was (supposedly) irrevocably committed. But for the Indonesian government the East Timorese response was 'anti-modern'—they were turning their backs on the (modern) nation, and reverting to a kind of tribalism. The same contradiction is to be found in the way different groups use the notion of Asian values. For the Indonesian government, East Timorese 'tribalism' constituted a departure from, and a threat to, both *Pancasila* and national progress. And for the East Timorese, modernisation, progress and its attendant values (respect for human rights, self-determination) were a means to an end, the 'end' in this case being, as far as Indonesia was concerned, an anti-nationalist and regressive political identity.

The contradictions inherent in this nationalist/modernisation bind were also apparent in the attitude taken to the incorporation of East Timor by Indonesia, over a 25-year period, by the Australian government. The latter did not oppose the move, mainly because it was felt that an independent East Timor would prove a 'destabilising influence' in the region: in this case, the 'Realpolitik' of modernisation and nationalism triumphed over the 'values of modernisation and progress' (such as the right to self-determination). The Australian government held this line until the Indonesian government agreed to a referendum on independence in 1999, which resulted in an independent East Timor with the withdrawal of Indonesian troops, administration and government.

GLOBALISATION, NEO-COLONIALISM AND ASIAN VALUES

We have covered two contexts of cultural politics in Asia so far: the role of the state and nationalism, and modernisation. The third context we will deal with is that of globalisation and neo-colonialism. The issue here is why the idea of Asian values is employed to justify 'locking out' or minimising western economic, political and cultural intrusions into Asian national sovereignty. One example of this, in the economic sphere, occurred when, as a result of the 1997–98 economic 'crisis', and following pressure from world financial organisations, South Korea was 'persuaded' to conduct a 'fire-sale' of its major corporations. In order to forestall this foreign 'buying up' of national assets, the Korean government used two approaches. The first approach was to dismiss bids because they grossly undervalued the corporations. The second was to appeal to the idea of Asian values: the government argued that if foreigners acquired Korean businesses, they would run them on an economic rationalist basis, without any regard for the welfare of Korean workers. This 'unfettered capitalistic approach' was contrary, they claimed, to the Asian way of running corporations, which involved looking after workers for life, in return for their loyalty.

The approach is also used to minimise or deflect the perceived impact of western culture and its accompanying values. In his 1994 'National Day Rally' speech, Goh Chok Tong, the prime minister of Singapore, referred to a Sustagen advertisement on Singapore television which showed a Chinese boy with a clenched fist saying 'Come on, Dad. If you can play golf five times a week, I can have Sustagen once a day'. The prime minister argued that an advertisement like this was inappropriate for the national values of Singapore because it would encourage children to be insolent to their parents. This didn't stay as simply a comment—the Ministry of Information and the Arts met with civic leaders and the advertising industry in Singapore to 'discuss ways to ensure that Asian values are not undermined in local advertisements' (*The Straits Times*, 26 August 1994). A major push was made to reaffirm 'family values'—love, care and concern; mutual respect; filial piety; commitment and responsibility, rather than individualism—as the dominant national values in Singapore.

The Ministry then released a statement saying that 'We should discourage advertisements which show Singaporean men, women and children behaving as if they were westerners' (*The Straits Times*, 26 August 1994), and new laws were introduced that allowed for the banning of foreign broadcast services and for broadcasters operating within Singapore (for example, Asia Business News, Reuters, HBO) to be licensed. Similarly, the American cartoon series *South Park* was banned from national television in Singapore, because it contains 'vulgar language', despite being available on the Internet to an increasing number of Singaporeans willing to download it. As one parent, who allows her 19-year-old daughter to view the Internet version, but not her younger children, said in an interview in *The Straits Times:* 'American society is more liberal, and young kids may pick up behaviour and language which is not socially acceptable here' (3 May 1999).

This is a familiar strategy in the government-controlled media in Singapore where a government position is presented by an 'ordinary' member of the public, in this case a housewife. This ensures that the policy of control remains, but the government is not always seen to be the 'bad guy'. The Singapore Broadcasting Authority currently blocks access to over 100 'unacceptable' (generally 'high impact' pornographic) Internet sites, although not *South Park*, recognising that 'It is not practical and almost impossible to block all offensive sites without impeding access to the Internet and its potential growth' (*The Straits Times*, 3 May 1999). Personally owned satellite dishes are not allowed in Singapore, however, and a very extensive cable television network has been put in place with access to all homes, thereby enabling far greater state control of television sources from outside Singapore.

Why is Singapore so aggressive in its championing of such values, and its control of information and media? There are two main reasons: the first is to enable the Singaporean government to remain in power. The Peoples Action Party has been in government since 1965: since independence, Singapore has effectively been a one-party state. But new strategies are constantly being implemented to enable the party to remain in power, particularly in the face of a more highly educated, and more western-influenced, population. This is also the case in many other Asian countries where one party remained in power for many years: the Golkar party in Indonesia, the Liberal Democratic Party in Japan and, until recently, the Kuomintang in Taiwan, with the United Malays National Organisation in Malaysia one of the few remaining in power today.

It is difficult to determine the extent to which this emphasis on Asian values in Singapore, and some other parts of Asia, is a reaction against western cultural and economic neo-imperialism, the symptom of a crisis in Asian nationalism, or a combination of both. John Kohut, writing for the *South China Morning Post International Weekly* (3 June 1995), argued that the most economically successful countries in the region were the most vocal in promulgating the rhetoric of Asian values. The argument was that the more successful they became, the more likely they were to be criticised by the West, and therefore the greater their need to find a philosophical underpinning 'for their preferred way of governing'. In other words, the invocation of Asian values could be understood as a response to, and a defence against, the 'orientalist' policies and discourses of the West. At the same time it also constituted, ironically, a parallel to orientalism. The demonisation of the West, and the dismissal of its supposed values (human rights, democracy, freedom of speech) was (and in some places still is) often used to justify the repression of 'enemies of the state', 'deviants' and various minority groups.

CONCLUSION

The production and promotion of the idea of Asia and Asian values can't really be evaluated as inherently good or evil, progressive or regressive. Rather it needs to be seen, in its many manifestations, as a symptom of the complexity of contemporary cultural politics in Asia: it is, among other things, one of the ways in which some states in Asia are attempting to cope with the three significant imperatives of modernity, postmodernity and postcoloniality. In our next chapter we will explain in more detail the relation between these three imperatives and contemporary Asia.

SUGGESTIONS FOR FURTHER READING

Birch, David (ed.) (1998) *Asian Values: Public Cultures*, a special double issue of *Social Semiotics* 8, 2/3

Clifford, J. (1988) *The Predicament of Culture*, Harvard University Press, Cambridge, Mass.

Milner, Anthony and Mary Quilty (eds) (1996) *Australia in Asia: Comparing Cultures*, Oxford University Press, Melbourne

Robison, Richard (ed.) (1996) *Pathways to Asia: The Politics of Engagement*, Allen & Unwin, Sydney

2

Modernity, postmodernity and postcoloniality

In his book on the cultural dimensions of globalisation, *Modernity at Large*, cultural theorist Arjun Appadurai devotes a chapter to the relation between modernity, colonisation and the sport of cricket in India (Appadurai, 1997). What Appadurai is particularly interested in is the way in which what seems like an altogether foreign cultural form, which should have been almost impossible to assimilate into local culture, ended up as such a significant aspect of Indian cultural identity. Appadurai is willing to try to explain the inexplicable. He writes that:

> It has something to do with the way sport is managed, patronized and publicized; it has something to do with the class background of Indian players and thus with their capacity to mimic Victorian elite values; it has something to do with the dialectic between team spirit and national sentiment, which is inherent in the sport and is implicitly corrosive of the bonds of empire; it has something to do with the way in which a reservoir of talent is created and nurtured outside the urban elites, so that sport can become internally self-sustaining; it has something to do with the ways in which media and language help to unyoke cricket from its Englishness; and it has something to do with the construction of a postcolonial male spectatorship that can charge cricket with the power of bodily competition and virile nationalism (1997: 91–2).

The list of contexts he provides includes public relations; advertising and the media; coloniality and class; the production of national sentiment; the dissemination of foreign cultural forms among the masses; the 'taking over' and reshaping of those foreign cultural forms and commodities; and, last but not least, foreign culture and gender politics. Although this list of contexts is put forward as a set of explanations for the place and significance of cricket in Indian society and culture, it can also serve as a departure point for making sense of the development of the relationship, at least at a cultural level, between the West and Asia.

We can carry the analogy further. Cricket is a prototypical western (actually, English) cultural form. The export of the game of cricket to India can best be viewed through the framework of the imperatives of colonial cultural politics. Two ideas are of particular importance in this context. The first is that the game may have been seen as being able to provide the colonising English with an activity which would make their lives easier and more enjoyable while away from home—cricket was a 'bit of England' in their lives in India. It could also be suggested that the camaraderie and discipline associated with the game was a way of keeping Englishmen 'English'—in other words, it would stop them 'going native'.

The English did not really expect that cricket (or any other English pastime) would actually 'civilise' the natives to the same level as themselves. However, there was an expectation that it might impart some level of order and civility among the natives. The photograph in Figure 3 of the Mayo College Cricket Team with its echo of the milieu of the English public school gives some idea of the process of dissemination of 'all that we of the British race regard as the most precious as principles of morality, loyalty and culture' (Lord Hardinge, Viceroy of India, on the occasion of the Annual Day of the Mayo College, 1913). These were some of the contexts of cricket in its colonial phase, and some of the ways in which the English thought the game would function in the colonies.

Once cricket was exported to India, however, a curious thing happened—something the English neither anticipated nor particularly welcomed. Firstly, India started becoming English—at least in the sense that sections of the population became addicted to cricket and cricketing culture.

Figure 3   The Mayo College Cricket Team, 1906

The second development, one that is still being played out to this day, is that cricket, of all things, ended up 'going native'. Cricket, which started out as a game played by 'gentlemen' like W.G. Grace, gradually became professionalised, and was taken up by countries whose teams were neither 'gentlemenly' nor, in all cases, white (Australia, India, New Zealand, Pakistan, South Africa, Sri Lanka, West Indies, Zimbabwe), and became intensely commercialised. This development was in no small way due to the extraordinary popularity and commercial success of limited overs cricket (distinct from 'test' cricket in that it is played over one day, rather than five) in India, Pakistan and Sri Lanka. In effect, cricket in the ex-colonies developed its own form of trajectory, influenced by local histories and cultural politics (see Srivastava, 1998).

What does all this have to do with contemporary Asia? The relationship between India and cricket is an example of the process whereby western colonialism and its cultural forms (which we can gather together under the labels of modernity and postmodernity) have both transformed Asian societies and cultures and, in the process, have themselves undergone transformations as they were picked up and used in specific Asian contexts. If W.G. Grace walked into an Indian cricket ground today, he would partly recognise what was going on before him, but he would be virtually illiterate with regard to the game being played (limited overs, colourful clothes, third umpires). Similarly, terms such as individual rights, citizenship, democracy and capitalism may seem unambiguous to some people, but they can undergo significant transformations once they are integrated into different social, political and economic contexts.

We can use this image of illiteracy, in the sense of not fully understanding something, in our approach to coming to terms with some of the ways in which discourses and texts, like a cricket match, may appear to be perfectly sensible to one person and be quite strange to another. In other words, there is no single, uncontested, meaning for these terms or concepts. 'Democracy' may mean one thing to many people in the UK, for example, but quite a different thing in societies like Pakistan, Indonesia, China or North Korea, which have a political role for the military which may seem quite alien to many other societies in the world. This role can transform democratic and parliamentary processes common in other countries, and often bring about western claims that there is no 'real' democracy in these countries. 'Real' in this sense is relative to a western definition of democracy which, in the hands of many western commentators on Asia, would suppose that unless the same pattern of democracy was established in Asia as, say, exists in the US, there is no 'real' democracy there.

In other words, concepts like democracy that have been exported to Asia by the West can continue to 'colonise' these countries if these terms are unthinkingly mapped onto Asian societies as if they were America or the UK. Cultural and social forms, as expressed in these key terms, therefore, can colonise just as much as people marching in and taking over a country. This sociocultural colonising is increasingly disputed by Asian leaders, particularly in countries like Indonesia, Singapore, Malaysia, South Korea and Taiwan, where one of the major transformations taking place is a desire to redefine some of these key sociopolitical concepts, like democracy and human rights, with an 'Asian' edge (see Anwar, 1996; Chan, 1997). What we are seeing increasingly across Asia, then, is the transformation of these terms and ideas—a process generally referred to as 'postcolonialism'. Postcolonialism is, therefore, a reaction to colonialism by processes of transformation which seek to replace and redefine the imported (colonising) structure or idea with structures and ideas specific to the sociopolitical and socio-cultural preferences of the country making the transformations (see Birch, 1995). The remainder of this chapter identifies and describes the main aspects of this process of postcoloniality (grouped under the categories 'modernity' and 'postmoder-nity'), and demonstrates its relevance to political, social and cultural issues in contemporary Asia.

MODERNITY

Modernity is usually understood as both a set of ideas or values closely tied to the European Enlightenment, and as a set of institutions, technologies, practices and politics. These ideas and practices are many and varied (see Gay, 1973; Turner, 1990; Giddens, 1990, 1991), but we specifically refer to the characteristics that were, and continue to be, transplanted to, or were appropriated by, certain parts of Asia.

What do we mean by the 'Enlightenment'? The Enlighten-ment was a period of western history (the eighteenth century) characterised by a number of developments, including:

- the partial replacement of religion by 'human' values (liberty, equality, fraternity, individualism)
- the rise of science and scientific methods
- a belief in reason, rationality and the civilising effects of culture and technology, and
- a belief in 'progress'.

These beliefs and values gave rise to new institutions and practices—forms of democracy, educational institutions, political parties and movements, nation-states—which were exported, in time, to all parts of the globe. The extent to which a people could be designated—by the West—as civilised came to depend on whether or not they subscribed to, and developed, the beliefs, values, practices and institutions of 'enlightened' modernity.

We can better think about the cultural aspects of the Enlightenment through an understanding of a specific manifes-tation of Enlightenment thought. The term 'modernism' itself comes to us from the world of art. The so-called modernist period of art in Europe is dated from around 1850 to around 1975. It is important to be aware of this modernist period as many of its artistic themes became generalised in western life: they became part of the way people thought the world ought to be, the manner in which societies should develop, the kinds of thinking and work western societies should valorise, and the kinds of things which could be identified as 'backward'. The themes of the modernists came to be generalised in everyday life in such things as modernisation theory in economics. As we will go on to explain, postmodernism as a category of thought sets itself up against many of the things it suggests were valorised under the heading of modernism and modernity. It is also important to understand the cultural history of modernism since much of current thinking about Asia, in both the West and in some parts of Asia, derives from early twentieth-century debates about 'backward' and 'progressive' thinking.

The art of the modernists—such as the Cubists, the Futurists, and the Constructivists—was an attempt to reflect the changes undergone by nineteenth-century European society: the developments in science and technology, the industrial revolution, the phenomenal leaps in communication technology and the mass production of mechanical goods. They wanted to deal with 'new' things, and they exhibited great optimism about the possibilities of scientific and technological advances. They wanted to paint the brave and exciting new world which, they hoped, was on the horizon. The modernists believed in such ideas as the forward march of history, the neutrality of science, and its ability to better the welfare of humankind.

The connection between modernism understood as an art movement, and the belief in modernity in general, should now be easy to see. The modernist valued science, technology, industry, the mass production of consumer goods, and the belief that humans (basically men at this time) could achieve anything they wanted with the help of 'new' methods. This belief in progress was, at the same time, a belief in the absolute superiority of western ways of doing things—in art, education, medicine, science, religion and, most importantly, in western 'forms of government'.

Probably the most significant European 'export', after capitalism, was the notion of democracy. Democratic government, as it is understood in the West, works, at least theoretically, through what we might call the 'abstraction' of the people. That is to say, people within western democracies are presumed to be free and equal individuals, rather than members of groups based on race, gender, age or class. Now historically this has never been the reality—women, for instance, have been denied their 'democratic rights' for centuries. Moreover, rather than being a government of 'abstract' individuals, democracies are comprised of various political parties and pressure groups (based on class, ethnicity, race, religion, cultural values) which compete against one another for the right to implement favoured policies.

What this means is that policy decisions are often 'compromises' which have to take into account a variety of different priorities and agendas. This form of government differs greatly from what preceded it in the West (monarchies, for instance), and from totalitarian or one-party governments which don't need to go through the same process of negotiating compromise policy decisions, or bothering with opposition parties. In a democracy the population is abstracted (in theory) in terms of free and equal individuality, each person being in a sense separate with his or her own desires and priorities; in one-party states the population is abstracted in terms of a supposedly shared set of values, beliefs and agendas, generally determined by the ruling party.

The history of western democracy is strongly informed by the development of liberalism and the notion of individuality (particularly as it manifested itself in the US), and the spread of free-market capitalism. Liberalism can be defined, briefly, as a general distrust of, and opposition to, strong state intervention in society, particularly in economic matters. This is the very opposite of what happens in one-party states, where individualism is seen as divisive and selfish, and economic matters are usually strictly controlled. The other two main features of modernity are the spread of capitalism and colonialism (see Ferro, 1997). The two are closely related, because the development of the notion of 'free-market' capitalism in the nineteenth and early twentieth centuries meant a move away, not only from government control and regulation of important economic matters, but from the notion of government responsibility to, and for, society or communities. In classical Marxist terms, the most important 'content' of the state—such as people and land—were taken out of the context of being part of a society or community, and became commodities in the marketplace. The logic associated with pre-capitalist societies and communities—which was to some extent informed by the notions of state interests, pastoral care and the maintenance of the fabric of society against violent ruptures and changes—was replaced with a capitalist logic of 'anything goes'.

The direct result of this change was that people and places were turned into commodities (see Ferguson et al., 1990). In other words, the defining characteristic of anybody and anything was what they could fetch in the market. This also meant a change in terms of who made decisions about social and economic policies. The logical extension of liberalism and the free-market economy was a move from direct and reasonably transparent state-based decision making (which would be determined by non-economic considerations) to a form of decision making arising out of a much more complex network of financial institutions that were not necessarily based in one state. States, to a certain extent, lost their political and economic autonomy, and came to be influenced in their decision making by international institutions.

Colonialism was, to a certain extent, driven by capitalism, whether in its endo (internal) or exo (external) form. Once groups of people came to be seen as commodities, then a range of policies was introduced which trained, regulated and constrained them in the names of their potential productivity and usefulness to capitalism and the state. The most obvious example of endo-colonialism in western Europe is probably those government policies and capitalist practices which gave rise to the industrial slums of nineteenth-century Britain. But the same capitalist logic, in tandem with national rivalries, directed exo-colonialist expeditions into Africa, Asia and other parts of the world. However, some scholars have pointed out that we should be careful not to generalise from this that the history of colonialism can be seen as simply an aspect of the history of capitalism in different parts of the world. This may lead to the perspective that 'colonialism as an economic and political formation [was the result of] an indigenous history of capitalist development' (Chatterjee, 1993: 31); and that 'colonial underdevelopment [comes to be seen] not as a process carried out by an external extractive force but as one integral to the peculiar history of Indian capitalism' (ibid.).

How do these various threads of western modernity (democracy, individuality, progress, civilisation, capitalism, colonialism) tie together? Markers of civilisation and progress (for instance, democracy and technology) became the criteria for deciding whether people could be exploited (based on the rationale that if they weren't civilised, they weren't really human) and the rationale for dominating them (they needed to be ruled by civilised peoples in order to become properly human). This notion of colonialist intervention and violence as a means of uplifting people was articulated, as mentioned earlier, in western culture, as 'the white man's burden'.

Modernity's ideals, and the technological progress that accompanied them, were supposed to produce some kind of utopia. But the reality was, and is, somewhat different. For example, the notions of 'universal rights' and equality were only ever applied to a small percentage of people. Women, the lower classes, and indigenous peoples (in Africa, America, Asia and Australasia, for instance), were not included. Moreover, the challenge 'to civilise' people was used as an excuse to dominate and enslave peoples who were designated as 'not civilised', simply because their cultures were different from (and therefore, the logic went, inferior to) the cultures of Europe. In other words, the so-called 'project of modernity' was largely Eurocentric, and made use of European technology to conquer non-European peoples, as well as using the development of different forms of knowledge to regulate and control the behaviour and practices of its populations (both 'at home' and in the colonies).

The French cultural theorist Michel Foucault makes the important point that forms of knowledge (usually based on scientific principles) produced by and for the state through newly developed fields and institutions (prisons, the police, education systems, the military) were used to produce specific ideas of what was normal or healthy behaviour (Foucault, 1997). This knowledge, and the discourses that articulated it, constituted a kind of policing of populations which extended to virtually all aspects of life (disseminated, as they were, through schools, the family, government policies and the media).

That policing continues throughout the world, including contemporary Asia. At the same time many western nations, because of the neo-liberal emphasis that is placed on individuality and the 'freedom of the market', have come to equate modernity with withdrawal of government from the social sphere. That is not the case in many parts of contemporary Asia. The diversity of contemporary 'appropriations' of modernity in many parts of Asia is consistent with regard to the diversity of sociopolitical and sociocultural contexts which has determined those redefinitions (see Chen, 1998; Yamamoto, 1995). Consider, for example, the following advertisements which featured as part of a government sponsored anti-AIDS campaign in Singapore in the late 1990s (see Figures 4 and 5). Advertisements like these would be unlikely to appear in most western nations, because they would be

Figure 4   Singapore Government anti-AIDS
advertisement, 1997

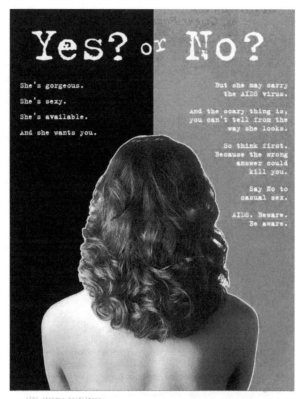

Figure 5   Singapore Government anti-AIDS
advertisement, 1997

interpreted as a violation of an individual's right to choose for themselves—a central tenet of modernist liberalism.

These advertisements are not suggesting how to practise safe sex in order to reduce the risk of AIDS, a common advertising strategy around the world predicated on medical and scientific advice about safe sex. They are actually instructing people not to engage in casual sexual relationships at all, a position that many in the West, and increasingly in Singapore itself, would interpret as a violation of their liberty and freedom to choose whatever lifestyle they wish for themselves. Liberty, in this sense, is therefore being redefined because of the sociopolitical imperative in Singapore to subordinate the

Figure 6   Tamil Nadu State anti-AIDS advertisement

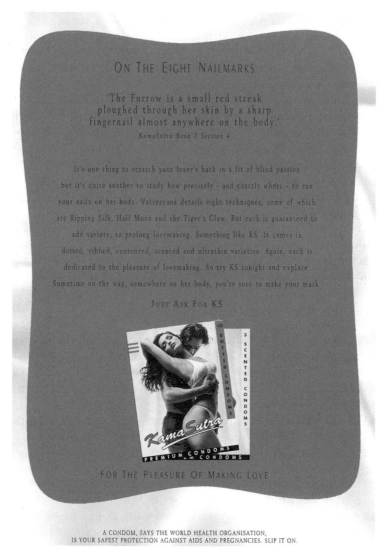

Figure 7   Kama Sutra Condom advertisement

role of the individual to the greater good of the society as a whole.

This is a common theme in contemporary politics in Singapore. It is economically inefficient to have people in hospital with AIDS, and complicated to promulgate a message about casual sex, which brings with it modernist notions of individual freedoms. The Singaporean government argues, however, that it is better not to allow such options, but to have a single position—'no casual sex equals no disease'. Western modernity is, in this case, brought under control and transformed, to suit the postcolonial priorities and values of contemporary Singapore. In that respect Singapore has established its own space for determining its identity (see Morley & Robins, 1995). Not everyone in Singapore (or elsewhere) agrees with this 'transformation' of modernity and its values, but what is important is to be aware of the rationale that informs it (see Chua, 1995; Hill & Fee, 1995).

This same scenario is being played out, in governmental and public spheres, in a number of states in Asia. Discourses which preach responsibility and communitarian values often circulate alongside more obviously westernised and consumerist representations. Consider the two advertisements shown in Figures 6 and 7, the first a two-page spread in the Indian magazine *Femina*, and the second from a 1997 issue of an English language newspaper widely distributed in India. The manner in which the advertisement for Kama Sutra condoms attempts to combine an internationally recognised aspect of 'Indian tradition' with contemporary notions of individualism and desire is particularly striking.

The advertisements, and the representations they employ, pick up on virtually diametrically opposed worldviews and values; woman as homemaker/sex object; sexual activity as bound by responsibility/unfettered; and the male subject of both advertisements as chivalrous gentleman/sexual tiger.

This opposition mirrors some of the tensions in Asia between advocates of communitarian values, and western-style consumerism and individualism. Tensions arise in many parts of Asia (and elsewhere) from a desire for 'developing' countries to benefit from the ways in which transnational, international and global corporations have increased the flow of capital around the world, and have technologised desirable information into products for easy consumption (see Garnaut & Drysdale, 1994). At the same time, however, there is an unwillingness to compromise their sense of who they are as an independent nation, by unthinkingly accepting the values associated with that flow of capital and information (see Drucker, 1993). George Yeo, Minister for Information and the Arts in Singapore, put it this way:

> We must make a clear distinction between free access to information and the right to educate. We need the widest access to information to educate our people, to bring in the latest technologies and to compete in a very competitive world. But free access to information does not mean letting the market decide what values we should have as a community. It is parents and teachers, not businessmen or journalists, who have the right to educate children. Thus, while we welcome greater and quicker access to the information available in the world, we must never concede our right to live in our own way and be different (Yeo, 1994).

Former President Soeharto of Indonesia sounded a similar warning to developing countries in Asia:

> The danger posed to developing countries is the flow of information from the West using high technology. In general they only seek profit and only adhere to mere freedom of the west which does not consider its effect on developing countries. We are determined to lessen the danger of cultural infiltration. If we do nothing our economies and cultures will be damaged (*Merdeka*, 15 April 1994).

Also consider, for example, a report in the 5 October 1997 issue of the popular Indian (English language) magazine *The Week* headlined 'Under the Greenwood Trees . . . No more kissing, says Mayor Shakuntula Arya', which is followed by an interview headlined 'We Should Not Tolerate Obscenity'. Shakuntula was complaining about young couples kissing in Lodhi Garden, a central park in India's capital city, and seeking a total ban on kissing in public places in Delhi. According to the report, 'Arya believes that public display of affection is an affront to Indian sensibility'. Some students at the Jawaharlal Nehru University in Delhi argued strongly against such a ban saying that 'Politicians have no right to doctor personal lifestyles'; while others, like Alka Lamba, President of the National Students Union of India, recognised that 'Though times have changed we still are not prepared to accept openness in our society'. As Shakuntula said:

> ... western culture is sweeping our youth away from our cultural moorings. What we are seeing today in parks is not part of Indian tradition ... In our culture relations are based on family values and have a permanence to it. In western societies when children grow up they are not kept at home, they are required to stand on their own feet and that leads to a lot of social problems. Their freedom has led to the degeneration of western societies (*The Week*, 5 October 1997: 26).

This story was picked up by one of the leading agencies (AFP) and circulated in the English language press in Asia under headlines like 'Outrage Over Delhi Plan to Ban Open Displays of Love', quoting Shakuntula as saying things like 'Such imitation of western morals does not suit our Indian ethos'. That ethos was to be sorely tested when a new satellite television channel called Plus 21 (owned by London-based ANC International) was launched in January 1998 with the sole aim of showing pornographic movies after 11 pm (in accordance with Indian broadcasting rules). And the Hong Kong based CEO of Rupert Murdoch's STAR TV (which is telecast by satellite into India) was charged in December 1997 with showing allegedly obscene films (for example, *Dance of the Damned*, *Stripped to Kill*, *Big Bad Mama* and *Jigsaw Murders*) which, it was argued, 'could damage India's social fabric'. What this makes clear is that the issue of what is obscene, or not, in India is not going to go away, as satellite broadcasting and access to more and more information sources from outside of India develop. As the AFP agency report on the new television channel put it, 'Open discussion of sex and steamy fare is frowned on in traditional Indian society' (22 December 1997).

Similarly, a popular teen singer in Thailand, eighteen-year-old Prissana Praisaeng (better known as 'Pooky') (who grew up in Australia and who, when four months pregnant, attempted to marry another (29-year-old) singer), sparked a debate about the evils of western influences on modern Thai values. Comments in the English language newspaper *The Nation* suggested that she was setting a bad example to other teenagers in Thailand; that she was too young to get married; that she should finish her education; and that she would set a trend among teenagers to get pregnant. Central to the issue was a lawsuit which Pooky filed against her mother who resisted the marriage—an action seen to be a western (and hence unacceptable), rather than a Thai thing, to do.

In another example, Anita Sarawak—a highly successful Singaporean (Malay) singer, now based in Las Vegas but who returns often to the region—was arrested in 1998 while holidaying in Malaysia with her fiancé, because she was sleeping with him in the same hotel room. She was considered to be setting a morally unacceptable image in Malaysia, and one which went against the 'accepted' norms and traditions.

The use of the rhetoric of tradition is a popular and widespread strategy throughout many parts of Asia, and is used in the context of domestic politics to good advantage. Whether or not this reflects reality is not really the important issue. What is important is the perception of it as a tool in arguing for social and cultural difference, and how this might be 'used' for political (and economic) national gain. What Anita Sarawak was doing in the hotel bedroom really wasn't the issue—what was important was the ability to stamp onto the public agenda, through this story, a reconfirmation of the sociopolitical imperatives of Malaysia as defined by those in power. Very similar issues were addressed with the long-running trial of the former deputy prime minister of Malaysia, Anwar Ibrahim, on sodomy, and other such charges. What is really happening is a redefining of the story in order to reconfirm in the public sphere those key principles of the postcolonial society which can clearly be seen to be different (often outrageously so when it comes to things like human rights) from the colonial exports (see Sardar, 1998). Postcoloniality is a key concept in developing cultural literacies for contemporary Asia, and needs to be understood within the context of both modernity and postmodernity and the struggles for cultural space in the region (see Wilson & Dirlik, 1995).

POSTMODERNITY

Postmodernity, like modernity, can be understood both as a set of ideas or attitudes (postmodernism), and a specific historical period with its own technological developments, cultural styles and political practices (see Docherty, 1993). Postmodernity and its various characteristics are related to modernity as developments and enhancements—through the use of more powerful and efficient technologies, more sophisticated and widespread forms of capitalism, the shrinkage of space/time, an increase in the electronic media, communication networks, and images and discourses—and as a reaction against its main principles, tenets and 'grand narratives' (such as the notion that the above-mentioned developments in technology and science were necessarily progressive and universally beneficial).

The most obvious difference between modernity and postmodernity is the phenomenon of globalisation, and the spread of global capital (Tomlinson, 1999). As the slave trade, the various trade routes of the ancient and medieval worlds, and colonialism demonstrate, globalisation is not a new phenomenon. However, in its contemporary phase, it can be understood as a combination of the following features:

Physical flows of people

Globalisation as a way of thinking was, in fact, stimulated by the mass migration of the past 20 years witnessed in North America and Europe.

Cultural flows

Examples include the spread in popularity of world music (Cajun, zydeco, quawalli, ska, juju, salsa, klezmer) and world foods; the diversification of religious beliefs; and the proliferation of non-English languages.

Information flows

This includes the so-called information superhighway, which supposedly offers instantaneous and almost unlimited access to information of all kinds—generally in English—and the information exchanged by people in an increasingly mobile world (such as travellers' tales and stories of immigrants when they return for a visit to their home countries).

The spread of the media and the increase of its influence

The proliferation and consolidation of global media empires means that people can watch *Neighbours*, *Dallas*, *Dynasty*, World Cup Cricket, Oprah Winfrey and so on in villages in Thailand, in slums in New Delhi and in high-rise apartments in Jakarta.

Flows of capital

This is linked to the previous two features. Flows of capital depend on, among other things, the smooth flow of information, and multinational media empires are an obvious example of global capital flows.

The flow of ideas

Information flows are not necessarily flows of ideas, if 'ideas' are reflections upon the information we receive. But information flows produce a degree of thought and awareness about ourselves, about others, and about the relationship between the self and others.

Globalisation is closely linked to global capitalism. We made the point earlier that modernity was characterised by a movement away from autonomous states and governments, and an increase in the influence, over state and international affairs, of financial institutions. This reached its apex at the end of the nineteenth and the beginning of the twentieth centuries, when financial institutions in Europe and America (and in particular bankers such as the Rothschilds and J.P. Morgan) were able to dictate to governments regarding both internal and external policies.

The period after the Second World War saw an extension of the influence of multinational and transnational corporations, mainly because of developments in communication technology, particularly computers (see Mattelart, 1994). Computers and other technologies have succeeded in decreasing the amount of time that is required to make decisions. There have been two significant results from this. Firstly, corporations no longer need to be centralised, or be predominantly located in any one place. On the contrary, they can be located across nations or continents, and continue to communicate and function without regard to the distances or time that separate them.

Secondly, decision making is becoming less and less the domain of centralised managers, and more and more tied up with the continuous retrieval of computer-generated information. One of the features of the various economic crises during the 1980s and 1990s has been the extent to which they have been influenced and exacerbated by computer-programmed investment strategies. That is, various institutions programmed investment decisions based on what is happening in short-term financial markets, but once things start going downhill, it is difficult for the situation to be corrected quickly.

The other pre-eminent feature of postmodernity has been the development of what has been called the 'information economy'. The quality of decisions made by governments or corporations depends very much on their ability to access reliable information as quickly as possible, to describe and analyse complex situations (economic, social, political), and to extrapolate decisions from that analysis. Ownership of, and access to, information has become the single most significant 'commodity' in the contemporary world. Tied up with these changes has been an opening up of world trade, which has helped transnationals and multinationals increase their share of national markets. While some nations have steadfastly refused to open up certain areas of their economy (the Japanese agriculture sector, for example, has been protected against foreign competition), the 1997–98 Asian economic crisis has changed things. In order to receive the aid packages offered by the World Bank and the International Monetary Fund, nations such as South Korea and Indonesia, which previously did not allow significant foreign ownership of their businesses, are being forced to allow foreign takeovers of Korean and Indonesian corporations.

Postmodernity can be understood, then, as a series of material changes and developments. But it is also characterised by a reaction against the notion, strongly associated with modernity, that material developments (for instance, in communication technology) are necessarily 'progressive', and universally beneficial. Postmodernist theorists argue that the unquestioning belief in the tenets of modernity and science has led, among other things, to the justification of colonialism, and the marginalisation of ways of thinking which may have been more beneficial for a larger proportion of humanity, but which were denounced as unscientific (traditional medical systems which do not require expensive medication, for example). This has happened not because modernity proved itself to be intrinsically superior, but because of the power and vested interests of those who promoted it. Hence, postmodernity also refers to a more sceptical attitude towards the key narratives of modernity, viz. science, and a more critical relationship with 'expert knowledge' in general.

POSTCOLONIALISM

There is a close connection between postmodernism and postcolonialism. Postcolonialism refers to the formal end of the colonial era when various countries in Asia, Africa and elsewhere became independent from European colonisers. Postmodernity—understood as global technological change, as well as ways of thinking about the world—has swept peoples, nations and localised communities into a new globalised world where it is extremely difficult to maintain any economic or even sociocultural autonomy, and in the process has altered many categories of thought. Along with the globalising of economies, there has also been a consequent globalising of culture. The spread of video, film, computer games, advertising, satellite television and the Internet, much of it originating from the West, has meant that western culture has largely colonised the world. That process carries with it specific cultural values, which compete against and often replace—as well as revitalise—local cultures and values (see Mattelart, 1996).

Much of this has been welcomed by non-western nations, which compete actively with the West in 'colonising' the world. Not all of the reactions are positive, however. Gobalisation has tended to decrease local and national autonomy, marginalise already disadvantaged groups such as casual and non-unionised labour forces, and even threaten or replace national sovereignty. The spreading of communication technologies means that governments have little or no ability to control what information is disseminated within their borders, since national borders can be easily bypassed by computer technology (see Bell et al., 1996).

Conventional colonialist practices involved overt violence and domination. In the nineteenth century colonised peoples were attacked by armies and navies, overwhelmed by superior military and other technologies, and enslaved or kept under political control. Postmodernity has seen a development of more covert forms of violence and domination, firstly through the continued influence, in colonised countries, of the 'overlay' of colonialism (institutions, language, political systems) and, more insidiously, through transnational and multinational corporations, world financial organisations such as the World Bank and the International Monetary Fund, and through the widespread dissemination of western culture. Although the age of colonisation has been replaced by what has been called 'postcoloniality', that 'post' refers not so much to an absence of colonising practices, but to their transformation (see Darby, 1997).

One example of this is the way in which colonial experiences continue to exert an influence over a nation's culture, institutions, identities and even their 'standing' relative to other 'postcolonial' nations, long after the colonial power has departed. Kuan-Hsing Chen quotes the Sri Lankan anthropologist S.J. Tambiah to the effect that:

> Sri Lankans are . . . apt to be proud and arrogant abroad: they feel superior to the Indians, the Malays, the Chinese, perhaps even the Japanese. For their eyes are set on the West, particularly Great Britain, which was their colonial ruler from the early nineteenth century until 1948. They are proud of their British veneer: their elites acculturated more quickly than their Indian counterparts; their island enjoyed a prosperity owing to its plantation economy that was the envy of its Asian neighbors; and the British Raj established a school system and a transportation system that, because of the island's size, was more efficient than any could possibly be in the vast subcontinent of India. And therefore, although India is their parent in many ways, all indigenous Sri Lankans—Sinhalese, Tamil, Muslim—become visibly annoyed, if not outraged, if Sri Lanka is mistaken physically to be part of India (Chen, 1998: 18–19).

More frequently, however, the combination of the effects of a colonial legacy, coupled with the ongoing practices of 'global postcoloniality', simply reproduces 'colonial relations' by other means. Renato Constantino describes American cultural influence in the Philippines as a form of:

> . . . systematic colonial brainwashing. History was mythologized to create an altruistic image of the American colonizer; our language was deprecated, our consumption habits were moulded to suit American products and our social and cultural life underwent a fast process of Americanization (Constantino, 1998: 57).

According to Constantino, American and, more generally 'northern' (involving 'developed' northern hemisphere nations such as Japan, and members of the European Union), colonialism is still carried on in the Philippines, only now under the guise of globalisation:

> The instruments of globalisation (are) . . . clearly manifested in the Philippines which is a model of a subcontracting state with virtually no independent national economy and existing mainly as a subsystem of Northern corporations. Whatever industrialization has taken place is due to the relocation of labor intensive and/or highly polluting processes of production from high wage countries of the North. The export industries which developed in the last decade or so— garments, electronics, handicraft, food processing, etc—have served mainly to supply the North with cheap labor-intensive-commodities (Constantino 1998: 61).

An even more insidious version of this continuation, by other means, of 'colonialist relations' between states produced one of the worst human-made tragedies of our time, the 1984 Union Carbide (UCC) disaster in the Indian city of Bhopal. The anthropologist Veena Das's (1996) analysis of the Bhopal disaster as a public event highlights an important aspect of the process of globalisation as a form of 'neo-colonialism'. Over two thousand people died as a result of gas poisoning caused by the leakage of methyl isocyanate (MIC) from the factory premises of the Indian subsidiary of the American-owned UCC in Bhopal. The aftermath of the disaster was that the suffering of the victims was forgotten, buried by the legal, medical, and bureaucratic arguments about who should take responsibility, and how much suffering had really been endured. The death and suffering of thousands of people was more or less 'wiped away' by legal and political dealings orchestrated by the company.

There was, then, and continues to be, a considerable disjunction between Enlightenment theories and ideals, which informed 'the project of modernity', and subsequent practices, policies and institutions—particularly so with regard to the question of endo- and exo-colonialism. If there is one area where the disjunction between modernist ideals and practices was (and still is) most obvious, it is in those countries colonised by European powers, all in the name of civilisation. The retreat of the colonial powers in the twentieth century, and the rise of national movements across what has been called the 'third world', may have brought to an end the era of colonialism, but there are serious issues still remaining with respect to neo-, endo-, exo- and postcolonialism in many parts of Asia.

GLOBALISATION AND ENDO-COLONIALISM

Many postmodernists view postmodern politics as a more subtle—but equally effective—form of (neo)colonialism, a maintenance of economic domination of people and nations through multinational and transnational companies and international institutions (the World Bank, the International Monetary Fund, and other institutions which provide financial assistance and economic advice on a global level) controlling media and communication networks, and disseminating ideology through western popular culture (see Ohmae, 1995).

But there are other, internal, colonising processes still taking place within postcolonial societies. While the promotion of Asia and 'Asianness' is often employed by Asian governments to hold back the global challenge to local economic and cultural autonomy, at the same time it can be used to control and marginalise the behaviour and rights of groups within a state. It is a form of colonialism, but it is directed internally, hence the name 'endo-colonialism'. The important point to understand here is that while there have always been examples of local exploitation in Asia based on class or caste, the introduction of western values into the social, cultural and political mix of a country has, in a sense, made those forms of exploitation more difficult to justify. The reaction against western values in different parts of Asia is often an excuse for certain groups to maintain their power over other groups—this is what we mean by endo-colonialism. One of the best examples of endo-colonialism involved the 'reclamation' of Hong Kong by China in 1997. Theoretically the Chinese government was freeing Hong Kong and its people from the control of British colonialism, but as Law Wing-Sang points out, the reality can be understood quite differently:

> Hong Kong was almost the world's last colony and 1997 was a watershed of the process of colonisation. Yet over the last years of transition few observers in Hong Kong failed to be amazed by this process, in which a glorious history was almost becoming an ironic joke. For the Chinese government, spurred by nationalist rhetoric, preservation of the status quo was a paramount concern. Always at odds with the colonial powers, the Chinese did not spare their vehement condemnation of the British government, particularly when it seemed to be uncooperative in the 'transitional' affairs of Hong Kong. In particular they stood firm to oppose any reforms that would alter past colonial practices. This was evident in halting reforms to make representation in the legislature wider. Curtailing social welfare provisions was another example (quoted in Chen, 1998: 109).

Another, less subtle, example of endo-colonialism can be found in the case of the Sudras of Rohini in India. Rohini is a large village in West Bengal which, according to a report in a leading Indian weekly English language magazine, *Sunday* (2–8 November 1997), under a banner headline of 'The Outcasts', practises a form of Hindu apartheid based on very old caste traditions which classifies certain people as untouchables. These people in Rohini earn their living from making and selling bamboo products, and despite the claims at Indian Independence that life would be much easier for the lower castes of India, and despite the fact that the government of West Bengal is Marxist in orientation, in many parts little has changed.

According to this report, the untouchables of Rohini, for example, still had to wear bells around their necks if they wanted to walk through the 'upper caste' area of the village—the bells warning the Brahmins, Vaidyas, Kayasthas, and other members of those castes that the Sudras were approaching. This way, they could avoid 'contamination' from the untouchables. The bells have since disappeared, but the 'untouchables' are still subject to considerable verbal abuse, and still have to live as far away from the upper castes as possible. They are not allowed in the houses of the 'upper castes'. If they do enter an upper caste house, for some reason or other, the house is washed and replastered with 'cleansing cow dung'. If they touch food, it is thrown away, and they are not allowed to draw water from the same well as the 'upper castes', nor are they allowed to enter the temple to pray. Despite a government literacy program, their children are discouraged from attending school, and if they do attend they are asked to sit together in separate classes. When asked about the situation, the 'upper castes' deny that such apartheid exists, but may accept that from time to time vestiges of the past may still surface—asking, for example, 'Do you have dinner with your servants at the same table?'.

Caste discrimination in India surfaces in many different ways: for instance, some groups have been driven from their traditional lands by property developers, entrepreneurs and tea garden owners. An example of this was highlighted in an issue of the widely circulated (both within and outside India) English language magazine *India Today* (15 December 1997), under the headline 'Savage Reprisal', and a subheading which stated 'Land disputes in a region mainly dependent on agriculture are driving landlords and peasants into an endless spiral of violence and retribution'. The article outlined a case in a village called Lakshmanpur–Bathe, in Bihar, where 2000 villagers were attacked by 250 armed men, in what the magazine referred to as 'caste cleansing'. At the end of the night 59 people in the village were dead. The magazine *Frontline* (26 December 1997) reported 63 dead, with a headline 'The Jehanabad Carnage', and featured graphic pictures of dead villagers.

This was not an isolated incident. What was different, perhaps, was that this village had not posted armed guards around its borders like neighbouring villages. The private army of 250 armed men, in the pay, according to both magazines, of the landlords, were part of a continuing program of harassment, based on the disputed ownership of 30 acres of land. Private landlord armies were formed in the 1970s and 1980s (often in response to 'revolutionary' left groupings such as the Naxalites, during the earlier period, and the People's War Group in the present era), and they have been strengthening ever since in some regions, leading to many similar incidents. In the sixteen districts which make up Bihar there were, up to October 1997, over 600 such incidents with almost 400 people killed. As *Frontline* puts it, 'What happened in Lakshmanpur–Bathe on that winter night was part of a long, bloody conflict between the haves and the have-nots of rural Bihar'.

Such activities are by no means confined to this—admittedly violent—region. There are militant groups representing a whole range of factions and fringes in India. The weekly magazine *Outlook* (22 December 1997) described such groups in an article headed 'The Serpent in Paradise', and cited the factional fighting between Muslims and Hindus which has seen many bombings and killings in the last few years. *Outlook* described the situation, in the fiftieth anniversary year of India's independence, as India finally 'united in the flames of communal violence'.

PROGRESS

Cultural politics in Asia is characterised by both these internal, endo-colonialist practices, and more subtle examples of neo-colonialism, where the values and practices of western Europe are put forward as 'civilising' gifts to a less than 'developed' (and therefore less civilised) Asia. Gift-giving can represent a particular form of power relationship and is not always done for purely selfless and philanthropic reasons. Failure to appreciate the gift can bring censure, as in an editorial written by Patrick Smith in the widely circulated *International Herald Tribune* (11 December 1997: 8) which pulled no punches in its denouncing of some forms of Asian democracy (the 'gift' given by the West). Under its headline of 'What East Asia really needs is more democracy', the article argues that:

> Under the social contract by which East Asian political elites rule, fast economic growth is conferred in exchange

for deferral of democratic government . . . [and that] East Asian nations are likely to emerge from their present problems either as more authoritarian or more democratic. It is difficult to discern much middle ground.

Smith sees the problem as one of leadership, suggesting that 'Their flexibility in the face of political and social complexity has been virtually nil'. There is a position developed here which quite clearly situates the political system of the West as superior to that of East Asia, and says, in effect, that to be more democratic really means to be more like the West. Smith argues that 'To one degree or another, these nations have never developed the strong supple democratic institutions they now need, and any future success will only come about with a new generation of leaders who have a broad, mature vision'.

This editorial naturalises one form of democracy, and one type of leadership, as the only appropriate one. What this presumes is that 'progress' and modernity can be equated, unproblematically, with western ideas or values, economic achievements and a market economy. However, if states derive their power not just from economic considerations, but from their sovereign capabilities, then such states do not operate simply as economic machines, but also as actors jealous of their territorial rights.

What constitutes that territory, for the most part, is what is driving many of the debates in Asia at the moment. These debates, and their various manifestations, including violence, form a process that is framed in many parts of Asia as a (post)colonial response to the development of modernity—where modernity is considered as traditionally 'owned' by the West. In a western paradigm of modernity, material achievement becomes the measure of modernity, and modernity is then the measure of civilisation. The tensions involved, and the memories of this phase, still drive the politics of sovereignty to be found in many parts of Asia.

CONCLUSION

In many parts of Asia, struggles to be modern may predominantly be about material achievement, but they are just as much about rejection of the privileging of western definitions of rationality. Understanding this is crucial to any understanding of postcolonial Asia. Seen in these terms the push for defining what is Asian about Asia (which regularly occurs throughout the region) is about determinations of sovereignty and renegotiations, not just of western colonisation, but of western definitions of modernity, rationality and civilisation.

Understanding this can put into context the sorts of comments made by Asian leaders such as the prime minister of Malaysia, Dr Mahathir, who has repeatedly called into question the potential (and actualities) of this sort of exo-colonial power. It also helps to contextualise some of the tensions (and paradoxes) involved in the anxieties of some Asian countries, and their attempts to construct 'morally authentic' Asian values and cultures (see Yao, 1994). It is this 'Asian essentialism' which is influencing some of the sovereign spaces of Asia once colonised by the West. Understanding this requires an appreciation of different cultural politics in Asia, and their relations to factors such as information flows and global capitalism, which are increasingly defining what constitutes modernity and modernisation in many parts of postcolonial Asia.

In our next two chapters we will describe in detail what is meant by terms such as globalisation, informationalism and the global economy, and explain how these concepts are impacting upon contemporary Asia.

SUGGESTIONS FOR FURTHER READING

Appadurai, Arjun (1997) *Modernity at Large*, University of Minnesota Press, Minneapolis

Castells, Manuel (1997) *The Power of Identity*, vol. 2 in his *The Information Age: Economy, Society and Culture*, Blackwell, Oxford

Chen, Kuan-Hsing (ed.) (1998) *Trajectories: Inter-Asia Cultural Studies*, in the series *Culture and Communication in Asia*, general editor David Birch, Routledge, London

Tomlinson, John (1999) *Globalization and Culture*, Polity Press, Cambridge

Turner, Bryan S. (ed.) (1990) *Theories of Modernity and Postmodernity*, Sage, London

3

Globalisation

In the previous chapter we suggested that what was happening—politically, economically, socially and culturally—in contemporary Asia needed to be read in terms of the contexts of, and the relations between, modernism, postmodernism and postcolonialism. In this chapter we will focus on the roles that culture plays in shaping and reflecting various identities—individual, local and national—in contemporary Asia, and how these roles and identities can be understood in terms of, and are shaped and transformed by, the processes of (and resistance to) globalisation.

Most of the significant aspects of modernisation, such as the development of the nation-state, were facilitated by cultural processes such as the widespread dissemination of printed texts, combined with massive advances in the number of people who possessed reading and writing skills. If we accept Benedict Anderson's notion that nation-states are really 'imagined communities'—that is, populations who come to believe and act as if they constitute a single, natural and more or less homogeneous entity—then we can say that the different states of Asia, even the most supposedly 'natural' and traditional ones such as China and Japan, have been 'culturally imagined' into existence.

This doesn't mean that other factors (military, economic, social) weren't important. But any political movement requires an idea to which it is committed in order to function effectively, and to bring 'the people' both into being, and along with it. Mao Tse Tung was partly right to say that power came from the barrel of a gun, but without an 'idea' of China (or at least a certain kind of China) being widely disseminated (through written texts, posters and, where populations were still largely illiterate, pictures and word of mouth) as its rallying point, there could not have been a successful communist revolution in 1949. Moreover, the existence of any political entity, in Asia or anywhere else in the world, depends on the maintenance of this sense of shared purpose, traditions, values, language and way of life—that is, it depends on the idea of a shared culture.

THE POLITICS OF CULTURE

By now it should be obvious that when we use the word 'culture' we aren't using it in the traditional sense of 'high culture'—poetry, opera, ballet and so on. We are using the word not to refer to specific genres or texts which are intrinsically valuable (for example, the *Mahabarata*, Tang Dynasty poetry, a Kurosawa film), but to texts of any kind (T-shirts, forms of dance, popular music, graffiti, sport, fashions, magazines, political cartoons, Buddhist scriptures) which are used, generally, to produce meanings and, more specifically (in Arjun Appadurai's terms), to 'express, or set the groundwork for, the mobilization of group identities' (Appadurai, 1997: 13). And, of course, one of the ways in which modern nation-states have attempted to communicate their identity, as well as to maintain social and political control over their populations (the two activities are very closely related), is by identifying and disseminating (through schools, pamphlets, media broadcasts) examples of 'national culture'.

For most of the twentieth century, nation-states attempted to regulate, control or influence the production of meanings—culture—within their boundaries, and this is still the case today to a certain extent. Many states have attempted to maintain this control because they have recognised the extent to which 'the production of meanings' (our first definition of culture) is able to 'express, or set the groundwork for, the mobilization of group identities'. Culture is one of the ways in which states facilitate their aims and objectives, and perpetuate their existence—think of the use Stalin made of Sergei Eisenstein's 'patriotic films' when faced with the threat from Nazi Germany, or the way Hollywood films 'backed up' the American war effort in the 1940s. At the same time, cultural texts can work to undo the authority of the state. For example, the most vehement public resistance to the Soviet bloc regimes came from writers and other intellectuals, and public opposition was often expressed 'culturally': the playing of jazz music, for instance, allowed Czech dissidents to get together without attracting too much suspicion.

As we have seen, one of the most important developments in the late twentieth century was the process of globalisation. In popular discourse, globalisation is usually understood as the way in which electronic technology—computer networks, satellites, fibre-optic cables—reduces the time it takes to send information, messages and images from one location to another, so that differences in space (countries, continents) become less relevant. There are a number of television advertisements (usually produced by telecommunications companies), which talk about a person conducting business in Tokyo, Seoul, New York, London, Singapore, Sydney, Los Angeles, Chicago and New York all in the one day—without ever leaving home (wherever that is). But there is a lot more to globalisation than just overcoming long distances to do business.

Globalisation also refers to a specifically cultural phenomenon—that is, the way in which that same electronic technology is able to disseminate cultural texts—films, television shows, sporting events, cartoons, music, pornographic images and stories, advertising, newspapers, magazines—across national borders. In some ways the first half of the twentieth century was characterised by a relatively regulated flow of cultural texts. If a government didn't approve of the messages, news or ideas found in a publication or film, it could simply refuse to allow those texts into the country. And since most texts were disseminated in hard copy, it was easy enough to control the 'cultural flows' coming from the outside, as well as oppositional discourses and texts being produced internally. Of course, this didn't prevent western nations, particularly America, from exporting their culture—Hollywood films, pop music, fashions and language—to all parts of the world, particularly Asia. Japan and the Philippines are perhaps the best examples of this phenomenon. After the Second World War, Japan integrated a great deal of western culture into its secondary education curriculum, and much of popular (and even 'serious') Japanese cinema (the Godzilla cycle, Kurosawa films and, more recently, the comedies of Juzo Itami), was based on Hollywood genres such as science fiction films. Virtually all of non-communist Asia has been culturally 'Americanised' to some extent.

The big difference between those examples of 'cultural imperialism' and what is happening with globalisation, is that even allowing for this western 'cultural saturation' of Asia, the state could at least theoretically control and regulate those cultural flows if it felt that local cultures were in danger of being swamped by imports, or if it disagreed with the ideas or values expressed by those cultural texts. Under the Soeharto government Indonesia, for instance, banned certain news-papers and journalists because it felt they were spreading 'disinformation'—in other words, they were expressing opinions and circulating news which the government wanted to suppress. Singapore has always strictly controlled cultural imports, banning anything which it feels promotes unhealthy lifestyles. For example, anti-AIDS campaigners in Singapore had a difficult time—they weren't really supposed to be able to discuss or write about homosexual activities, because that was interpreted by the government as promoting homosexuality.

Globalisation can alter this situation because the state's ability to regulate or maintain surveillance of cultural flows is weakened. If a nation-state wants its communication networks to be up to date then it has to allow many of its citizens—such as secondary and tertiary students, and business people—access to the Internet. Once a company such as News Corporation's Sky Channel is 'allowed to operate' in a country, then the state can't really control what is shown, or said. Both of these devel-opments offer citizens access to new ideas and values which might call into question the nation's laws and policies, the authority of the government, or the viability of the state. And there is almost nothing the state can do about it. Singapore has, to a large extent, managed to retain some control over its media by banning personal satellite dishes and introducing cable tele-vision access into every home in the country; but with the exception, say, of Macau or Brunei, no other country in Asia is small enough to be able to make this option logistically (or economically) possible (see Birch, 1998b).

We tend to think of globalisation as an effect and feature of modernisation, but really it is something else—it is both postmodern and anti-modern. Remember that one of the main features associated with modernity was the development of a number of institutions—in areas such as government, health and education—which took as their central function the care, surveillance and regulation of populations. And the institution which largely controlled these other regulatory institutions was the state. Of course there has always been a certain amount of capitalist involvement in these areas, but by and large responsibility for the population—how it was governed, its health, its education—lay with the state. Globalisation, as well as disseminating cultural texts almost instantaneously across the globe, has changed the way we understand the field and practices of economics and finance.

Whereas nation-states once exercised relative control over both their cultural and economic spheres, now cultural and economic flows tend to move across and through states—witness the speed with which, in 1998, various Asian currencies were devalued because of fluctuations—which they were powerless to control—on the international money markets. One of the effects, then, of globalisation is that those institutions which were set up to control and organise populations and their activities (cultural, economic and social) have either had their authority eroded, or have become increasingly irrelevant. Globalisation has ushered in a new, postmodern, world which is largely market-driven, has little or no respect for national boundaries or borders and, because everything is effectively tied together by transnational systems and networks, is subject to a kind of chaos theory effect, whereby a crisis in one country (political instability in Indonesia, say) can precipitate a crisis in other parts of the world (Japan, Taiwan or Australia).

TURNING TO 'THE LOCAL'

Globalisation has in a sense replaced, or is in the process of replacing, modern Asia with postmodern Asia. But there is another side to globalisation which doesn't fit in so neatly with this narrative of 'the triumph of the global'—what we might call a turning to 'the local'. We have seen how the nation-state produced itself as having a kind of monopoly over a whole range of activities (politics, economics and, of course, culture).

What this meant was that most signs of cultural difference within populations (languages, traditions, rituals, values, religions) were either replaced by a state authorised 'culture', or relegated to the status of 'curiosities', quaint 'local cultures' which could be brought out to show tourists—itself a form of what we have called 'endo-colonialism'. For example, the criticisms made of the use of the Karen people (see Figure 8) and some advertisements for Malaysian tourism (see Figure 9), are good examples of the ways in which a specific 'local' culture can be exoticised (and turned into a commodity) for tourist consumption.

These two examples are informed by the same kind of cultural politics: the hilltribe people from Myanmar and the Iban chieftain are both reduced to versions of what *The Straits Times* article refers to as 'prisoners in a human zoo'—they are indistinguishable from the 'thick jungle', 'awesome caves' and orang-utans awaiting western tourists.

These and other 'local' cultures (such as 'local' religions, political movements and religious groups) were politically de-authorised by the nation-state—it is as if one 'ethnic' group gained control over other populations, and then pretended that their culture represented everyone. This scenario has been acted out in Asia, more or less consistently, since the success of the great 'nationalist' movements of the twentieth century (in China, India and Korea, for example) and, most particularly, since the end of the Second World War (in Taiwan, Indonesia, Tibet and Vietnam, among others). However, the conditions which allowed this kind of 'cultural monopoly' to exist—or at least pretend to exist—are exactly the conditions which have suffered under globalisation. Once it becomes impossible for nation-states and their institutions and bureaucracies to monitor and control everyday cultural practices, ideas, values and meanings, then 'local cultures' can come out into the open, although like 'official cultures' they still have to contend and compete with the threat of incoming global forces (see Perera, 1995).

RESIDUAL COLONIALISM

Since the Second World War various Asian nationalist movements had wrested control of their own affairs, effectively

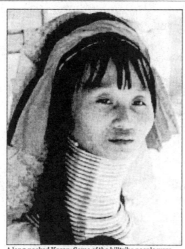

Long-necked Karens won't be used in sell-Thailand drive

BANGKOK— The Tourism Authority of Thailand (TAT) stressed it has no policy to use long-necked Karens as a selling point to promote the Amazing Thailand tourist campaign in 1998-1999.

TAT Governor Seree Wangpaichitr's remark follows a recent article "Prisoners in a human zoo" published in The Times newspaper which criticised opportunists for violating the human rights of Karen tribes by parading them for the benefit of tourists.

The hilltribe people in question are migrants from Myanmar living in three refugee camps at Ban Nam Phiangdin, Ban Huay Seuthao and Ban Nai Soy in Mae Hong Son province.

The Karens were reportedly led away by a man who took them to a tourist spot in Ban Tha Thon, in Mae Ai

district, Chiangmai, for an exhibition.

Tourists reportedly paid between 250 and 300 baht (S$9.50 to S$11) each to view the Karens.

Mr Seree confirmed that the northern tourist agency, Mae Hong Son and Chiangmai provincial authorities have not supported the parading of the Karens to draw tourists to the region.

The authorities had never ignored the human rights of these tribes people as alleged, he said, adding that the Chiangmai authorities were now preparing evidence to take legal action against operators who had abused the rights of Karens.

The Karens would be taken to refugee camps in Mae Hong Son and have their work permits revoked to avoid being exploited by selfish operators, said Mr Seree.

A long-necked Karen: Some of the hilltribe people were reportedly paraded in front of tourists. — File picture.

Figure 8   *The Straits Times*, Singapore, December 1997

putting an end to old-style colonialism. However, there were two factors which ensured that the West still exercised control or influence over Asian politics, social life and culture, even after the success of the various independence movements. The first of these is what we could call the effects of 'residual colonialism'. The Indian political scientist Partha Chatterjee has argued, for instance, that the forms nationalism took in Asia, and the kinds of states that were produced by those nationalist movements, were largely the products of a 'westernised imagination' (Chatterjee, 1993). In other words, the western educated and influenced upper- and middle-class elites who drove the various Asian nationalist movements transposed western cultural, social and political structures, practices and values onto and over local cultures, more or less suppressing them as the western colonialists had done before them. And if we look across Asia, we can find many examples of how western cultures—particularly American culture—have 'taken over' from 'local' cultures.

Now, of course, this notion of unfettered and all-conquering western cultural imperialism has to be qualified. As we explained earlier, India may have adopted cricket from the days

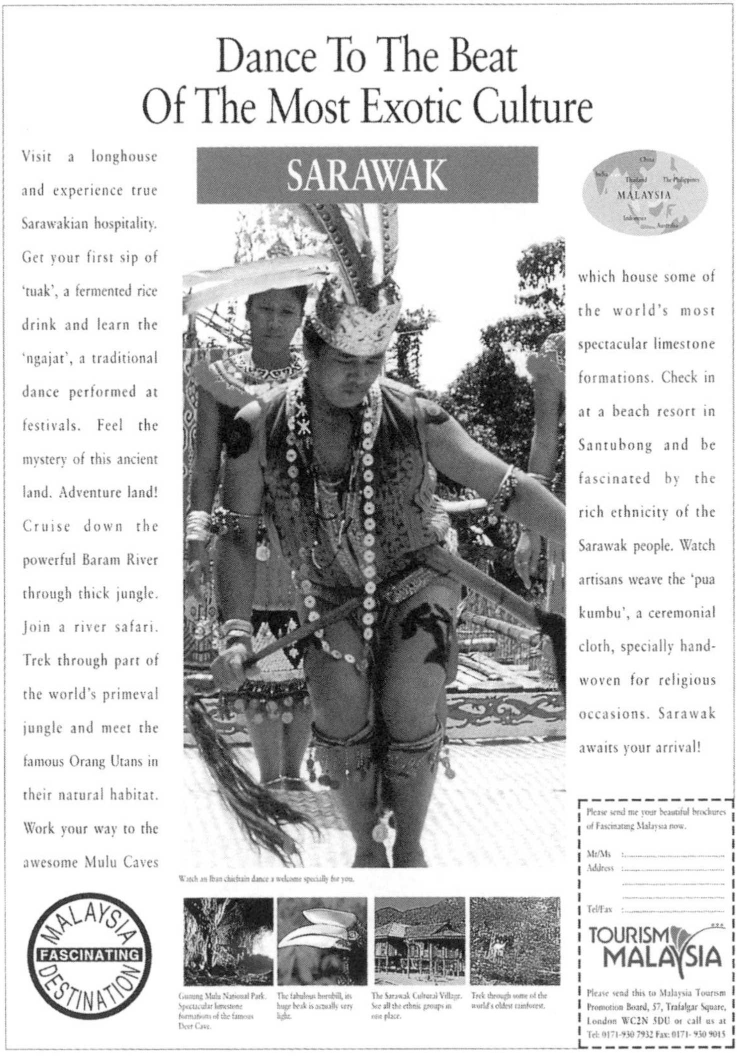

Figure 9   Tourism Malaysia advertisement, 1997

of the English Raj, but what they did with it, and what became of it, is entirely another matter. Many Asian cultures have obviously borrowed heavily from, say, American popular culture, but they have adapted it to their own ends. Kurosawa's film *Yojimbo*, for instance, may have been heavily influenced by the Hollywood western, but it is altogether different from any

American film—it deals with 'local' issues and values (in this case, among other things, the modernising and westernising of Japan). American popular cultural texts have become 'cultural vehicles' for representing and working through non-western ideas, meanings, identities and issues—such as the influence of the West on Asia. Films as diverse as Hsui Hark's *Once Upon a Time in China* and Ang Lee's *Eat Drink Man Woman* are examples of how Asian directors have taken up western cultural genres (the action film or the sitcom) and used them as a means for representing contemporary cultural and political issues (the handover of Hong Kong, cultural values and the generation gap in contemporary 'westernised' Taiwan).

With globalisation, then, the rules of the game of 'cultural exchange' may be tilting far too heavily towards the West. But there is nothing about globalisation, as such, that demands this current western imbalance, as Japan's recent domination of various aspects of technology worldwide has demonstrated. Globalisation, like the cricket match in India, the invasion of East Timor by the Indonesians and the films and other examples we have referred to so far, can be treated and read as texts, and as such need to be treated with the same critical awareness that recognises that there are power relations involved in the positioning of certain meanings as more impor-tant (valorised) than others. As such, there are people responsible for these positionings—agents of meaning making—that make one thing more important than another. So, while it may be valid to suggest that the imbalance in cultural exchange in contemporary globalisation patterns springs from the notion that many people in Asia have an 'in-satiable appetite' for all things western (American films, Italian fashions, French wines), it is also important to recognise that the agency of the electronic media is largely owned and controlled by western companies, and, as such, there will be a flooding of western cultural texts (and their accompanying images, ideas, meanings and values) into many countries in Asia, which will be more or less helpless to resist this 'western homogenising' of both official and more 'localised' cultures.

Cultural theorists, for instance, point to the work of the French sociologist Jean Baudrillard, who has traced the demise, in the West, of cultures that have some connection with local times and places, and their wholesale replacement by what he calls 'hyper-real' cultures, as exemplified by Disneyland (Baudrillard, 1993). For Baudrillard, every period and place, and their accompanying cultural texts (everything from medieval castles to Viking ships to Nazi leather outfits) can be, and are being, substituted for any other period—people can live in a Tudor house, an American backwoods log cabin, or a Spanish hacienda, and dress like a 1920s flapper, a 1940s bobby-soxer, or a flannel-suited 1950s businessman. What many cultural critics in Asia fear is that this 'mass substitutability' of cultures brought on by the processes of globalisation will overwhelm many cultures in Asia and usher in a new period of western 'cultural domination'—a new form of colonialism.

Why should many cultural critics (and some politicians and bureaucrats in Asia) be so concerned about the possible mass substitution of national and 'local' cultures by a homogenising, globalised western culture? The answer lies with the two definitions of culture we provided earlier in this chapter—anthropologically speaking, culture can be understood as both the production of meanings, and relatedly, that which expresses, or sets the groundwork for, 'the mobilization of group identities' (Appadurai, 1997: 13). We made the point that nation-states were more or less created through the 'mobilisations of people' by certain ideas, predominantly by the idea that they shared a common identity with some peoples, and were different from others.

The markers of this group identity were usually cultural—people spoke the same language, practised the same religion and shared a cultural heritage (literature, dance, history, music, songs, traditional dress, rituals). Take one obvious example: the 'idea' of China is inconceivable without reference to, and is usually exemplified and articulated in terms of, stories, texts, narratives, sayings, conventions and rituals of behaviour, and cultural genres (particular kinds of music, painting, poetry). Every politician who attempted to both 'mobilise people' in the name of the Chinese nation, and legitimate their own right to speak and act in the name of the people—from Sun Yat Sen to Mao—did so by positing some kind of 'organic link' between themselves and China's history and culture.

Every nation-state in Asia is based on, and legitimates itself in terms of, what we could call 'official ideologies'. That is to say, every successful political movement or group which 'became a nation' (or, in the case of political parties in China, North Korea, Singapore and Taiwan, 'stood in' for the nation) took cultural texts and 'made them mean' what they wanted them to mean. Again returning to China, in the Guandong State Museum there are copies of historical and literary texts from China's ancient past which chart the rise and fall of dynasties, governments, emperors, warlords, generals and popular leaders. Accompanying these texts are commentaries, presumably provided by museum officials, which help visitors read—that is, make sense of—these texts. The commentaries could be reduced to two 'master narratives'—these ancient texts were explicable either in terms of demonstrating the determination of the Chinese people to throw off corrupt and despotic rulers, or to resist and defeat foreign invaders. The real 'referents' here, however, were not ancient battles or popular movements, but the victory of the Chinese Communists over the Kuomintang (now fled to Taiwan), and the ongoing 'hostilities' between China and the West (particularly the US). The authorities took these cultural texts and 'filled them in' with their own meanings like 'the communists were the rightful heirs of all true Chinese patriots, and would defeat foreign enemies'.

An example of the artificiality of these 'nationalist narratives', or at least of the way they can be 'politicised', can be found in the situation of the 'two Koreas'. In an inteview with the American cultural theorist Fredric Jameson regarding the question of Korean unification, Paik Nak-chung points out that:

> While we are in many ways still a single nation with a long history of unified life and an acute sense of that history, we have had two virtual nation-states for over forty years now, with two almost diametrically opposed social systems, and therefore with very different individual and collective experiences (quoted in Wilson & Dissanayake, 1996: 363).

The point is that although there seems to be the basis for a single Korean 'imagined community', the two political systems and their accompanying discourses and values (for instance, capitalism versus communism) produce two different, and largely incompatible, versions of Korean history and identity (see Birch, 1996).

All nation-states try to 'fill in' and control the meaning of cultural texts. In a globalised world, however, this is just about impossible. 'Foreign' films, television shows, news broadcasts and Internet sites, many of them emanating from the West, provide a steady and largely unavoidable stream of stories and meanings which are often quite contrary to the 'official' meanings disseminated by the state. As we pointed out earlier, when the word 'democracy' is used in Malaysia, South Korea, Singapore, Pakistan, China or Vietnam, it will be 'made to mean' different things—emphasis might be placed on the citizen's responsibility to the state, on group interests taking precedence over those of the individual, or on the importance of having stable, uninterrupted government. But when people in these countries watch foreign news broadcasts or films, they find that democracy means something else—individualism, unfettered market forces, and the right to bear arms.

However, it is far too simplistic an assumption that contemporary nation-states have been completely unable to place any kind of check on the 'foreign' cultural and media flows. In fact, Asian states have made vigorous efforts to police their 'borders' in this context through ensuring as much as possible that debates on new technology and information flows are carried out within a national policy framework. So, the Asian 'satellite service market remains a market developing within the boundaries set by state controls' (Leonard & Harrison, 1997: 6). Manifestations of this include current debates in India, Taiwan and Malaysia on the Indian Broadcasting Bill of 1997, the Taiwanese Television Law and the *Malaysian Broadcasting Act* respectively. The Indian Broadcasting Bill, for example, requires that, with some exceptions, those wishing to operate satellite services be licensed. And, although the degree of actual control varies, Asian governments have also been able to exercise it to some extent through 'licensing satellite operators and the ownership of receiving equipment' (Leonard & Harrison, 1997: 6).

CULTURE AND HABITUS

Foreign cultural texts, particularly electronic texts which are difficult to censor or regulate, basically pose a challenge to the authority of nation-states because they do away with the state's ability to 'narrativise' and guide the behaviour and lives of their citizens. But what do ordinary people make of these cultural texts, and how do they influence and affect their everyday lives? In order to address this question, we will make use of the theories of Pierre Bourdieu, and in particular his notion of 'habitus' (Bourdieu, 1991).

'Habitus' can be understood as a set of values, dispositions and practices which are behind just about everything we do and think, but which we have naturalised, and made unconscious. For instance, the sense of space that mid-western Americans are used to, and feel comfortable with, has no real intrinsic value— for other groups it might be seen as a massive waste of space. The point, for Bourdieu, is that we come to accept these values as natural, to the extent that they drive our behaviour, and the ways we understand ourselves.

Bourdieu argues that people's activities and behaviour are shaped by their cultural 'trajectories' (their parents, the schooling they received, religious institutions they were involved with, whether they came from working- or middle-class backgrounds), and the various 'fields of activity' they work in or come into contact with. Bourdieu suggests that every institution or field has its own authorised language (what Michel Foucault calls 'discourses'), as well as specific values, ways of doing things, expectations, hierarchies, dress codes and meanings. In order for a person to 'fit in' and progress (for instance, be employed and promoted in a business or bureaucracy) people are required to more or less 'unconsciously' adjust themselves to the institution or field they are in.

The same applies, of course, to the relation between a state and its population. Official cultural texts promote ideas and ways of behaving that in a sense compete with 'unsanctioned' or 'unauthorised' cultural texts and their meanings. However, in those countries in Asia where there is no apparent discrepancy between official and unofficial culture (Singapore, Malaysia, Indonesia, North and South Korea, Vietnam, Burma, Taiwan, China and Cambodia for example), the habitus of a person remains reasonably stable. That is, the idea a person comes to have of themselves, and how they understand their relation to social, political, economic and cultural institutions, is usually remarkably durable, and can survive essentially intact even as it undergoes minor transformations (brought on by a change of job or marital status, or the replacement of one government leader by another).

This is still true, although to a lesser extent, in those countries in Asia which have a relatively *laissez-faire* style society, economy and culture, such as the Philippines, Sri Lanka and India. Even when there is no overt government control or regulation of the flow of cultural texts (and meanings), the habitus of people is maintained in a number of ways—through the influence of religion (such as Catholicism in the Philippines and Hinduism in India), through schools and other educational institutions and, in particular, through the various private and public media. What happens in these countries— as with western democracies—is that cultural texts and meanings flow in a reasonably free and uninterrupted manner. However, there is a sense in which different institutions more or less replicate one another in terms of the meanings associated with 'capitalised' ideas. In the West, for instance, the notion of the importance—even centrality—of the individual, as opposed to, say, socialist notions of the pre-eminence of group interests, can be found across fields as varied as the media, universities, and economics and finance, as well as across most other groupings (economic classes, for instance). What this means is that the cultural texts and meanings that are produced in these kinds of states may promote all kinds of different ideas and values, but generally speaking this 'variety' can always be recuperated (a text that promotes homosexuality, for example, is living proof of the tolerance of democratic states, and their respect for individuality and difference). The baseline is that in *laissez-faire* states a person's habitus may be subject to modest transformations but, as in the case with more 'regulated' states, it remains remarkably durable.

We have argued that a person's habitus can tolerate social upheavals, and moving from one field to another, because there is a 'continuity of meaning' throughout most national cultures (usually promoted by governments, in concert with major institutions). How does globalisation affect this? Arjun Appadurai has suggested that the more or less unregulated flow of cultural texts, in concert with the continuous 'flowing of peoples' that characterises contemporary Asia, works to 'move the glacial forces of the habitus into the quickened beat of improvisations for large groups of people' (Appadurai, 1997: 6). He builds on the work of the French theorist Michel de Certeau (de Certeau, 1998) to argue that people in the contemporary world are continuously confronted with images, narratives, information, voices and perspectives from all corners of the globe that don't equate with the 'received ideas' of their habitus. Rather than having stable identities, people have to 'make do' with whatever is at hand, so to speak—they can borrow identities from Hong Kong Kung Fu films, American sitcoms or Indian melodramas. This means that they necessarily are distanced not just from 'official' cultural texts and their meanings, but from any institution or text which claims to have a monopoly on meaning—simply because, in a globalised world, what is understood as normal is always subject to (very rapid) challenge and change.

What is clear, then, is that there is no single set of outcomes of the various forces—cultural, political, economic—that we have referred to as globalisation. The most important thing to remember is that social and cultural change is always a contingent process; that it is dependent on a range of actually existing human practices. Consider the following two contrasting examples of 'local' responses to the processes of globalisation.

The first example comes from the sphere of interaction between Balinese culture and non-Balinese systems of knowledge, in this case, the allopathic medical system as represented by the doctors and the hospital system in Indonesia. The anthropologist Mark Hobart notes that Bali has a long history of interaction with the west, having served, among other things, as an imagined paradise, the site of Dutch colonialism, a theatre of war, and the object of mass tourism (Hobart, 1995: 59). So quite clearly the idea of an 'authentic' Balinese culture which has remained the same for millennia is somewhat problematic. Cultures are always in a state of flux, and always a mixture of influences. Despite the proliferation of western medical knowledge, and the implicit state support it receives due to its perceived superiority over traditional systems of healing, many Balinese continue to patronise traditional healers for many of their health problems. Doctors trained in western medicine, Hobart says, 'do not explain what they are doing or why [and] treat the patient as passive and ignorant' (60). In contrast, 'the local healers . . . [involve] their clients as co-agents in inquiry into the causes of their condition' (60),

thereby giving the patient a sense of involvement and empowerment. Now, the healing 'consultations', while 'traditional',
are not simply expressions of an unadulterated Balinese
culture, rather they concisely represent the interaction of
cultures:

> Balinese had been greatly taken with television footage of
> missiles pursuing aircraft around the sky during the Falk-
> lands war. And the healer made use of such 'modern' images
> in her diagnoses. (On another occasion she likened the form
> of attack on a victim to a radio-controlled device.) She also
> showed that she was familiar with Indonesia and the basics
> of clinical terminology, which she encompassed as part of
> Balinese healing practice (Hobart, 1995: 62).

The second example provides a quite different picture of the
consequences of cultural interchange. The Sora are an indigenous population group who reside on the border between the
Indian states of Orissa and Andhra Pradesh. Until the 1970s,
Piers Vitebsky notes, shamanistic practices were quite prevalent in many aspects of Sora life, and the service of shamans in
conducting funeral rites and healing rituals were frequently
sought. In fact, 'a number of children and young adults were
learning to become shamans' (Vitebsky, 1995: 185). By the
mid-1990s, however, Vitebsky found Sora society had very few
shamans, and some important shamanistic rituals were in the
process of being abandoned. Vitebsky suggests that a reason for
this lies in the way shamanism was perceived as fundamentally
connected to the local landscape. Many aspects of everyday
life, the Sora suggest, are affected by the inclinations of the
dead—whose spirits become part of the landscape, especially
which crops are grown—towards the living. With the incursion
of the market economy into Sora society, however, the 'soul-
force' which resides in crops is exported out of the locality, 'to
be eaten by strangers' (187). In effect, then, with the inclusion
of 'outsiders', the cosmological world posited by shamanism—
the relationship between the Sora, their ancestors, and the
landscape—became increasingly untenable. The inclusion of
the 'outside' world in this case has led to the situation where 'a
vital link between people and their environment is severed'
(187), with the consequential decline of the supporting belief

system. So, here we have an instance of the erasure, rather than adaptation, of a 'traditional' practice in its interface with the global cultural and political economy.

CONCLUSION

Up to this point we have dealt with the ways in which Asia is being influenced by the cultural dimensions of globalisation. But many countries in Asia, as we have seen, are also vulnerable to the vagaries and changes of the global economy. Electronic business and commerce, information technology, financial services and tourism, and the knowledge economy, in particular, are likely to become much more important in developing economies in Asia as part of a global knowledge economy, particularly in the regional groupings of countries in East Asia, South Asia and Southeast Asia. As such, understanding contemporary Asia, against the backdrop of a global economy which, more and more, is governed by the rapid flow of information, is becoming increasingly significant.

It is apparent, then, that globalisation poses a threat, in Asia and elsewhere, both to the sovereignty of the nation-state, and to the viability of some 'local' cultures. But this does not necessarily mean a homogenising of all culture. On the contrary, as the authority of the sovereign state is diminished, this may allow 'local' cultures that have been buried by the state to emerge—a process often referred to as glocalisation. Globalisation, then, is likely to pave the way for a new kind of cultural 'imagining' which, although producing something far less durable than the habitus of the past, is potentially far more flexible.

In our next chapter we will consider how contemporary Asia is being transformed by two of the other 'driving forces' of globalisation—informationalism and global capitalism.

SUGGESTIONS FOR FURTHER READING

Featherstone, Mike (ed.) (1990) *Global Culture: Nationalism, Globalization and Modernity*, Sage, London

Featherstone, Mike, S. Lash and R. Robertson (eds) (1995) *Global Modernities*, Sage, London

Huntington, Samuel P. (1997) *The Clash of Civilizations and the Remaking of the World Order*, Simon & Schuster, London

Scott, Alan (ed.) (1997) *The Limits of Globalization: Cases and Arguments*, Routledge, London and New York

Wilson, Rob and Wimal Dissanayake (eds) (1996) *Global/Local: Cultural Production and the Transnational Imaginary*, in the series *Asia-Pacific Culture, Politics and Society*, general editors Rey Chow, H. D. Harootunian and Masao Miyoshi, Duke University Press, Durham and London

4

The information age and the global economy

In this chapter we look at how contemporary Asia is being influenced and changed by some of the economic aspects of globalisation. There are two major areas we discuss—the characteristics of what has been called 'informationalism', or 'the information age', and, more or less as a consequence of this, the development of the global economy and the transformation of capitalism.

Informationalism can be understood in terms of changes in communication technology which have placed information—and its production, circulation, identification, retrieval and application—at the centre of contemporary economic activity. This change has a profound effect on the field of economics and finance, producing a global economic system which has redefined what we understand by labour and capital, financial processes, the extent of government control of currency rates and other local economic factors, and the very idea of capitalism itself.

There are four main characteristics identified by Manuel Castells (Castells, 1993) that, when taken together, can be said to constitute informationalism. The first of these is the different communication technologies that have been developed from the 1970s onward in the areas of computing, telecommunications and microelectronics. These technologies have revolutionised communication: their speed of operation, and ability to store and relay information, place them in a different order from their precursors (primitive computers, telephones, television). They have effectively succeeded, as far as communication activities are concerned, in compressing time and making space increasingly irrelevant.

Secondly, what makes these technologies even more effective than previous communication networks is the development of a common digital language which can integrate different modes and fields, creating interfaces which allow for an unrestricted flow of information, not only across national borders, but from one set of technologies (say, telecommunications) to another (computers).

Thirdly, information and knowledge are no longer simply the means to various other 'productive ends'—the production of goods, for instance. Rather, they are now both means and ends—information and knowledge are now principally applied to developing more effective and faster processes for producing, retrieving and transmitting information, and for integrating different communication circuits.

Fourthly, the distinction between people and machines and their roles in communication and information production is being diminished—increasingly, what we are looking at is a form of informational 'cyborgism', where every aspect of human activity (politics, business, sport, gambling, education, entertainment, shopping, sex) is dependent on, and facilitated by, communication technology.

GLOBALISATION AND CAPITALISM

This 'age of informationalism' has given rise to a globalised economic system characterised by these changes. Corporate productivity, profitability and competitiveness now depend on the speedy generation and application of information—something which is accentuated by the fact that competition (for markets, developing new products, networking, attracting capital investment) now comes from all over the world. To cope with these and other changes, many corporations have been forced to globalise their operations, so that the cycle of production and consumption is no longer tied to local or certain transnational spaces, and many forms of corporate activity (management, recruitment of labour, capital attraction, advertising, communication networking) are carried out, directly or through surrogates, on a global scale.

Largely because of informationalism, capitalism has, since the 1970s, undergone radical reforms and changes, all of which have had important consequences for both labour and the sovereign states in which corporations are nominally located. Corporations have responded to the new era of 'global competitiveness' (and economic uncertainty), firstly, by attempting to increase both the profitability and productivity of capital and labour and, secondly, by becoming more flexible with regard to core businesses and activities. The global economy functions in a way that is both dependent on, and analogous to, the integrated communication networks we referred to earlier. Because the different areas and components of the field are interconnected (local and international corporate offices, stock exchanges and currency markets) business activity takes place twenty-four hours a day. Capital 'never stops working', whether in stock markets, investment funds or banks. Huge amounts of capital are invested, relocated, accumulated, devalued, lost or withdrawn across the world every few seconds—which can have a serious, and sometimes catastrophic, effect on corporations, markets, regions, nations and the global economy itself. Corporations have attempted to adjust to this uncertainty by becoming more 'flexible' in their operations—which means the replacement of stable, long-term employment (usually paid at union-negotiated rates) by short-term, poorly paid jobs (either through mass redundancies or, more dramatically, by shifting whole operations to more 'suitable' labour markets)—and by replacing large numbers of jobs in traditional areas (for instance, manufacturing) with technology and smaller (and non-unionised) workforces.

There are two important—and in a sense conflicting—political consequences of this development. Traditionally, many sovereign states in Asia have identified, promoted and aligned themselves with local corporations against international rivals, either directly (by restricting access to local markets and providing subsidies to local companies), or indirectly (by manipulating tariffs and quotas). As a consequence, corporations have identified with and entered into a form of 'social contract' with the local communities from which they drew their workforces—for instance, by providing tenured employment and subsidised accommodation.

Even the Hong Kong government, which supposedly

adopted a *laissez-faire* policy in this regard, played a significant role from the 1950s onward in facilitating and developing local businesses through leasing crown land cheaply to businesses, subsidising public housing and, less directly, through significant increases in government expenditure on housing, education, health and social welfare (Castells, 1998: 258). However, it may well now be true that the potentially catastrophic consequences (for regions or nations) of massive electronically driven movements of capital (which could produce failed businesses, depreciated currencies, high unemployment and political instability) make it imperative that sovereign states align themselves with, influence and also support national corporations. This is notwithstanding the fact that the other side of the globalising of the economy is that corporations are increasingly becoming less 'national', less committed to 'local' interests and communities, with decisions about policies and directions often being made 'somewhere else' (see Vatikiotis, 1996).

Although global capital flows and fragmented management structures have changed some of the relationships between a number of corporations and states, labour markets have not yet undergone the same level of 'globalisation'. While corporations are now either spatially or virtually global, there are obvious restrictions (in terms of logistics and immigration rules) which have limited the extent to which labour can imitate the movements of capital flows or management 'dispersals'. And yet a number of changes are taking place with regard to labour, the most obvious being the willingness of corporations to relocate themselves in areas where cheap, non-unionised, or well-educated labour is available. Another change is that, to a certain extent, labour is becoming more mobile and transitory, both on an individual and a mass scale. The availability of new jobs—most of which are likely to be short-term and relatively low-paid—is dependent on global economic conditions, and the vicissitudes of individual corporations.

When corporations decide to relocate, either in search of cheaper, non-unionised labour, or because they have diversified their activities and require an appropriately educated workforce, labour tends to follow, whether from other parts of the nation, or from different nations. This has accentuated what has been described as the contemporary 'diasporic phenomenon', in which masses of people travel to foreign areas, and set up their own 'homes away from home', in search of employment. Corporations are, to a certain extent, selecting their staff from pools of highly educated labour across the globe, particularly where there are local shortages, or employment costs are relatively high. And finally, because both production systems and management are often located globally, there is a tendency for corporations to employ less educated and cheap local labour. All these changes not only constitute significant departures from traditional patterns of labour employment, they also work to alter the 'national' nature of a corporation (see Thurow, 1996).

An interesting example of the changing nature of labour employment is a US case of what could be referred to as the satellite office. An American company that provides stenographic services to hospitals in the US set up an office in India in order to utilise the large pool of inexpensive (by US standards) English-language trained stenographers and transcribers that exists in that country. Through this arrangement, doctors operating in theatres in a US hospital are able to directly dictate procedures undertaken during an operation (the recording of which is required under US law) to satellite-linked stenographers in Delhi, and have transcripts forwarded later. A similar arrangement is in place in India's 'silicon valley', in the South Indian city of Bangalore, where software experts supply services to their US-based clients through electronic mail. Call centres are a similar global phenomenon: customers may make a local phone call to request a service, order a product or make a complaint, unaware of the fact that the call could be re-routed to another country, where labour is cheaper, and the call completed there.

THE POLITICS OF THE GLOBAL

The combination of informationalism and globalisation has produced a global economy—and a politics to go with it. Renato Constantino, for example, writes that in the Philippines in the 1970s:

> . . . the government exerted efforts to combat the control by transnational corporations of the local drug market. The latter were dominant because they owned the patents, thus

preventing Filipino drug manufacturers from producing these patented medicines at lower costs. Actually, what the foreign drug firms were doing was just importing the products from their mother companies and packaging them in the Philippines, reaping huge profits through their transfer price arrangements between principal and subsidiary. The government's efforts to alter the situation met with strong opposition not only from foreign drug corporations, but also from their respective embassies. When under the Aquino government laws were passed that sought to challenge the monopoly of the transnationals, lack of efforts from doctors undercut the effort to popularize cheaper, generic drugs. Moreover global firms were able to adjust to the law and even gain from the new trends ushered in by it. They are now engaged in the manufacture of natural and herbal medicines, many of which are based on indigenous knowledge (Constantino, 1998: 61).

Central to this politics is the diminishing ability of sovereign states to completely manage, control and in some cases even influence their own economic, social, political and cultural affairs. States have become less powerful in certain areas because the contemporary basis of most economic and political power is predicated on an ability to consistently renew and control information and information technology (see Ohmae, 1991). Power has passed, to some extent, to multinational and transnational corporations (although these, too, are vulnerable to changes in capital flows and the volatility of the currency markets) which are unlikely to be closely aligned with specific sovereign states. This is evident in the economic sphere, where many important decisions are 'made elsewhere', firstly at an anonymous global level (for instance, by stock and currency markets), and secondly—when a state runs into difficulties—by various global economic bodies such as the G7 states, the International Monetary Fund, or the World Bank (see Neher, 1991).

The important point to consider here is that the great 'Asian economic success stories' of the last three decades (Japan and the so-called 'Asian tigers'—Singapore, Taiwan, South Korea and Hong Kong), as well as some of the more 'developing' Asian economies (Thailand, Indonesia, Malaysia, Vietnam) have all, to a large extent, based their economic growth on strategies and policies which are antithetical, and more or less incommensurate, with regard to the workings of the global economy (see Dobbs-Higginson, 1993). The alignment between state and business interests we referred to earlier was characterised by strong government intervention in the economy in the form of loans, subsidies and policies which helped foster growth. But there were other critical factors, such as the maintenance of political 'stability' and continuity, industrial 'peace' (which kept labour costs down) and the protection of national markets from external competition (which allowed countries such as Japan, and later South Korea, to achieve considerable trade surpluses with the US and Europe). These conditions were achieved in different ways in different countries (contrast, for example, the 'business/labour accord' in Japan with the often brutal repression of unions in Taiwan and South Korea), but tended to have the same effect.

DEVELOPMENTAL STRATEGIES

Manuel Castells (1998) cites Japan as the prime example of this 'developmental strategy', and he goes into considerable detail in order to explain how this state/business alignment worked in practice. Japan, like Taiwan and South Korea, benefited from US military protection after the Second World War (which meant it was relieved of the burden of military expenditure), and was ruled for a long period by the same political party (the Liberal Democratic Party), which facilitated the development of a powerful network involving government members, bureaucrats and business leaders. The most important aspect of this network was the Ministry of Finance, which used its two major arms, The Ministry of International Trade and Industry and the Bank of Japan, to control and guide virtually every significant economic-related activity, such as the control of credit, export/import allocations and technological development. The 'Asian tigers' benefited from the same kind of 'state guidance' in the economic sphere (although this was often accompanied by and achieved via considerable political repression). Singapore, for instance, took strategic decisions to educate its workforce, restrict immigration, subsidise housing, repress unions, restrict individual rights and political diversity, assimilate new information technology and diversify its economy (moving from traditional manufacturing areas to high technology such as semiconductors and microelectronics, and more recently to financial services), seeking to attract high levels of foreign investment in partnership with the government. Similar policies were adopted in Taiwan and South Korea and, to a certain extent, in Hong Kong.

In this respect, the economy, then, becomes more important than the people themselves, with arguments developed by those in power justifying repression and subjugation of individual rights in the name of developing economic well-being. These arguments are well rehearsed throughout many parts of Asia and it is important to recognise in any understanding of contemporary Asia that these arguments are often now naturalised as part of the sociocultural habitus (see Wu et al., 1997).

The success of Japan and the 'Asian tigers', and the economic development of Indonesia, Malaysia, Vietnam, Thailand and, most significantly, China, gave rise to the notion that the Asia–Pacific basin would dominate economically during the last decade of the twentieth century, and well into the twenty-first. Castells is extremely sceptical, however, that there is such a thing as an integrated Asia–Pacific economic region along the lines of the North American and European trade blocs (Castells, 1998). He acknowledges that there is a closely integrated pattern of production (much internal Asian 'trade' is what he describes as 'trans-border exchanges' from one multinational's location to another) and investment (one-third of Japanese investment, for instance, is in China). He points out, however, that the high level of non-Asian investment in, and penetration of, Asia, particularly China (currently the centre of world investment), has only succeeded in integrating Asia more fully into the global economy.

There are a number of other factors which have facilitated this process of global integration. The most important of these is the enforced opening up of the Japanese, South Korean, Chinese and other previously protected markets to the rest of the world: these countries had partly financed their continued development by internally reinvesting trade surpluses, but those trade surpluses were being threatened and eroded by other countries and trade blocs taking action against Asian protectionism, as well as by the high value of currencies such as the Japanese yen. At the same time, and as Singapore's continued success demonstrated, there was a need for countries such as Japan, South Korea, Hong Kong and Taiwan to both seek new markets for their products, and diversify their production base. Rising internal labour and production costs also induced corporations to set up plants overseas, in order to take advantage of cheaper labour and local market knowledge. All these factors have moved many economies in Asia away from relative economic autonomy and into situations where they are subject to the vicissitudes of the movements of global capital, the opening up of markets, and the dismantling of the internal conditions and networks which contributed to their comparative success. In Japan, for instance, stable labour conditions, based on the notion of tenured employment, have given way to increasing unemployment and job insecurity which, as a consequence, loosened the Liberal Democratic Party's grip on power, and discredited and eroded the influence of institutions such as the Bank of Japan.

Perhaps the most significant aspect of the integration of Asia into the global economy has been the 'opening up' of China to capitalism, foreign investment and contemporary communication technology. Communist China seems an unlikely player in the global capitalist game, but since the 1970s, when Deng Xiaoping introduced an 'open door' policy, and again in the early 1980s, with the designation of four 'special economic zones' to attract investment from outside, China has been headed, inexorably, down the path of at least limited integration into the global economy. And, as a result, China has attracted a great deal of interest from global financial markets and corporations, which see its one billion person market as potentially sustaining and driving the global economy, and soaking up a great deal of global overproduction, in the twenty-first century (see Dirlik, 1994).

Global capitalism has not had an easy time accessing this market: China wants foreign investment, markets and technology, but the Communist Party is wary of the impact globalisation could have on the ability of the Party to maintain social and political control of the country, and on the prospect of a western 'takeover' of Chinese corporations and markets. Interestingly, most of the foreign investment in China has come, via Hong Kong investment funds, from the overseas Chinese sectors in Taiwan, Singapore, Thailand, Malaysia, Indonesia, Australia, Canada and Hong Kong, and to a lesser extent from Japan (Castells, 1998). This 'Chinese network' of investment is predicated on business networks mainly working at provincial levels, and is usually facilitated by local party bureaucrats (see Ong & Nononi, 1997).

'Chinese capitalism' has succeeded to the extent that China is the fastest growing economy in the world, and runs high trade surpluses with both the US and Europe. However, there are a number of difficulties that threaten the state's ability to maintain its communist/capitalist juggling act. Firstly there have been a number of social consequences of opening up the economy: high levels of unemployment, failed local companies, mass migration from country to urban areas and the effective dismantling of the welfare state have all combined to produce a potentially volatile scenario. And of course China, like other countries in Asia, is extremely vulnerable to the consequences of capital flows, currency fluctuations and market overproduction which devastated South Korea. On the other hand, the spread of capitalism 'threatens' to produce a significant 'middle class' which could challenge the Party's control of the civic sphere in China—although the example of News Corporation's back-down, when pressured by the government, on running BBC News on the STAR television channel, suggests that the state is acutely aware of the significance of telecommunications and the need to control information flows. However, the extent to which this can be achieved within a state that is becoming more integrated into an information-driven economy and culture is becoming more of a problem.

This 'problem' was evident well before the Asian financial crisis of 1997–98, but since that time the full ramifications—economic, social and political—of the integration of Asia into the global economy have become more evident. The short-term economic and social effects of the crisis were catastrophic—the Indonesian rupiah, for instance, lost 75 per cent of its value, countries went into recession, property and stock values were slashed, foreign debt increased because of the weak state of local currencies, and unemployment rocketed. The political and social consequences were equally devastating. Indonesia experienced widespread food shortages which led to violent anti-Chinese riots, and President Soeharto was deposed. Governments fell in

South Korea and Japan. In Malaysia Prime Minister Mahathir, who in September 1997 had criticised currency dealers for speculating against the ringgit (currency dealer George Soros called the prime minister a 'menace to his own currency'), eventually withdrew the ringgit from currency markets. This precipitated a falling-out between the prime minister and his deputy, which provoked further political unrest, both in Malaysia (in the form of anti-government protests), and in terms of Malaysia's relations with Singapore and Indonesia (which had criticised Mahathir's handling of the crisis).

Although a number of Asian countries (China, Taiwan, Singapore) emerged relatively unscathed, the integration of Asia into the global economy can be said to have precipitated a bout of economic 'neo-colonialism' on the part of the West towards Asia. The most obvious example of this was the reaction of the International Monetary Fund (IMF) to Indonesia's economic crisis: the IMF agreed to lend Indonesia the finance it required to continue paying off its creditors (mostly western financial institutions), providing Indonesia accepted and implemented a range of harsh economic policies, which caused considerable suffering amongst the people, and in the process created further political instability. Much the same happened in Thailand and South Korea. On a more general level, the crisis virtually opened up Asia for a takeover by western finance: local markets were freed up, assets were undervalued, protectionist policies were withdrawn and Japan was pressured by the G7 to open up its markets to take in the overproduction of goods from other Asian countries (such as South Korea), and to more or less dismantle the 'developmental' economic framework (alignment of state and business, tenured employment, government direction of research and development investment) that had been in place since the Second World War.

Of course there have been other, more positive aspects of the crisis—for instance, the move towards greater political freedom in Indonesia and South Korea. At the same time the twin factors of informationalism and the globally integrated economy have worked to largely renew the threat of western economic hegemony in Asia, producing widespread suffering, unemployment and political instability, and, perhaps temporarily and only in some states, reducing the level of sovereignty to superficial levels.

TECHNOLOGY AND THE CONTROL OF MEANING

The other consequences have been in the area of telecommunications, which plays a crucial role in the production and dissemination of discourses, news, images, information and ideas. With the widespread deregulation through much of Asia (but not, for instance, in China) of telecommunications, the ability of states or governments to control the messages and images that are crucial to the production and maintenance of 'imagined communities' is considerably reduced (see Birch, 1998a, 1998b). Perhaps the best example of the conjunction of global economics and the politics of 'information flows' has occurred in Malaysia, which was politically destabilised by the rift between Prime Minister Mahathir and his former deputy Anwar Ibrahim. Although there were various political rivalries and contexts which contributed to the falling-out between the two, the main point of difference was the issue of Malaysia's integration into the global economy. Anwar, as Finance Minister, not only presided over Malaysia's integration, but, despite Mahathir's misgivings, after the Asian crisis broke and the ringgit collapsed in value he introduced an IMF-inspired austerity package (involving cuts to government spending, increasing interest rates and controlling credit) designed to assuage the global markets. These measures merely produced a recession and widespread suffering.

Mahathir blamed Anwar and his financial advisers. He placed one of his own confidants, Daim Zainuddin, in charge of the economy, and effectively got rid of Anwar and the governor of the Central Bank, an Anwar supporter. Anwar was eventually arrested in September 1998, charged with and subsequently convicted of various sexual offences: his supporters (predominantly drawn from Malaysia's large Muslim population) staged protests which resulted in violent confrontations with the police. But the most interesting aspect of the split between the two men concerned the struggle to control and disseminate information and meanings about the events. Mahathir was strongly supported by the local media, which he effectively controls. But Anwar supporters, and other Malaysians interested in hearing or reading Anwar's speeches, logged onto various websites in order to collect information (which was then physically posted on bulletin boards throughout the country), or used satellite television or computers to access foreign press accounts (which were generally hostile to Mahathir). People were arrested for 'spreading disinformation', attempts were made to close down websites and Mahathir attacked the foreign press's coverage as being designed to destabilise Malaysia, while serving the interests of global capitalism.

CONCLUSION

The kind of 'crisis' we have been discussing, both economic and cultural, is facing many states in Asia which, to some extent, need to commit themselves to the global economy in order to reap the benefits it can provide (investment, access to markets, technology), but at the same time are faced with the loss of control (economic, social and cultural) that goes with the concomitant 'liberalisation' of the civic, political and cultural spheres of the state. This process can be read, on the one hand, as an opportunity for marginalised and repressed groups to gain some level of political autonomy, and for the development of an educated and liberalised 'public sphere' free of state control or manipulation. On the other hand, global economics and informationalism can be read as the reimposition by 'other means' of western hegemony (economic, political and cultural) in the Asia–Pacific region. In our next chapter we will look at how these conflicting issues are being 'played out' in the public spheres of contemporary Asia.

SUGGESTIONS FOR FURTHER READING

Castells, Manuel (1997) *The Rise of the Network Society*, Blackwell, Oxford

Kelly, David and Anthony Reid (eds) (1998) *Asian Freedoms: The Idea of Freedom in East and Southeast Asia*, Cambridge University Press, Cambridge

Ohmae, Kenichi (1991) *The Borderless World: Power and Strategy in the Interlinked Economy*, Harper Business, New York, rev. edn, 1999

—(1995) *The End of the Nation State: The Rise of Regional Economies*, HarperCollins, London

Wu, D.Y.H., H. McQueen and Y. Yamamoto (eds) (1997) *Emerging Pluralism in Asia and the Pacific*, Hong Kong Institute of Asia Pacific Studies, Hong Kong

5

The public sphere

Until the 1997–98 financial crisis destabilised the South
Korean, Indonesian, Malaysian and Thai economies, and
threatened to take Japan with it, the Asia–Pacific had been cele-
brated and praised for showing the West, and the rest of the
world, how to achieve and sustain high levels of economic
growth. The economic 'great leap forward', not just of Japan but
of states such as Singapore, South Korea and Taiwan, was
consistently presented as the model the rest of the world should
follow. Just exactly what this model was has been the source of
some contention. For sociologists such as Manuel Castells, the
success of the 'Asian tigers' was based, to a large extent, on
government intervention in, and active promotion of, local
industries and corporations. But as Castells (1998) and others
have noted, this economic development often went hand in
hand with government policies, strategies and initiatives which
worked to maintain domestic political and social 'stability',
often at the expense of other, sociocultural 'freedoms'.

The success of these 'developmental strategies' relied on the
integration of the economic, political and social spheres of the
state. All three were equally important. Economic success, of
course, enabled the state to provide the technology, infrastructure and services which kept the financial juggernauts going,
but it also contributed to social and political stability (in the
form of higher wages, employment, better health care, education, housing, transport and the availability of a wider range of
consumer goods) which helped minimise social discontent.

This was an important consideration, given that so many Asian states had backgrounds of relatively recent political instability, authoritarianism and violence—conditions hardly conducive to providing the kind of ongoing stability required to achieve and maintain economic growth.

However, in this context of developmental economics, what tended to be pushed well into the background in many countries of the region was the notion of 'the public sphere'. By this we mean, following the work of Jurgen Habermas, that set of forces which operate in society to throw into focus 'democratisation, public participation and oppositionality' (Lim et al., 1995: 5). Much has been written in recent years on the notion of the public sphere, most particularly with reference to race, gender, sexuality and equal opportunity issues, these issues bearing down most sharply on how meaning might be publicly negotiated in society.

Historians, political scientists and cultural analysts point to two important aspects of recent political and social history in Asia as being central to the success of some of Asia's developmental states. The first of these was the widespread identification of a single political party with the state (the Kuomintang in Taiwan, the Liberal Democrats in Japan, Golkar in Indonesia, the PAP in Singapore), which produced an 'authoritarian' or, at best, a 'limited' form of democracy. This allowed political parties to integrate with, and shape, government bureaucracies, business groups, the judiciary and other areas of civic society. The second aspect was the widespread promotion, even in ethnically heterogeneous states (such as Singapore and Malaysia), of communitarian values (which privilege the community over the individual), coupled with the implementation of strategies for resolving or heading off ethnic or other forms of divisive conflict. The key to these successes has been the state's ability to monopolise political power, and control the production and dissemination of meanings and ideas—for instance, popular debates about national values, state policies and political decisions. In other words, the relative social and political 'stability' that has characterised Asia's developmental states in the last two decades was tied to their ability to regulate and control, contrary to the rules and practices of conventional democracies, both political apparatuses and the public sphere.

DEMOCRACY AND THE PUBLIC SPHERE

We pointed out earlier that democracy was one of the most important legacies of western colonialism in Asia. However, in order to understand how that has been taken up in various Asian contexts, we need to look at the characteristics that set democracy apart from other political systems. In particular we need to appreciate how it ties in with, and is dependent on, the notion of 'the public sphere' to balance or provide a check on the extent to which people are 'governed' by the state.

With monarchies, and authoritarian governments, a society is equated with a single identity. Democracy, however, supposedly removes the possibility of any identification between a single party, or person, and the state. Prior to democracy, power was incorporated in the person of the monarch whose place is guaranteed by God: pre-Second World War Japan and contemporary Bhutan are two examples of this. With democracy, the site of power becomes an empty place—no-one has any God-given right to hold on to power, or to set themselves up as 'standing in for' the state or the people. Consequently, there is a split between the spheres of power, knowledge and the law. This gave rise to an unending process of social 'questioning'—from opposition political parties, but also, importantly, from the people.

This questioning of governments and political power by 'the people' is strongly associated with the notion of liberalism. French theorist Michel Foucault (1997) argues that liberalism developed as a response to the strongly interventionist policies developed in the German states in the eighteenth century. Liberalism ushered in a significant change of direction for governmentality because it broke with the 'reason of state' which had emphasised interventionist policies aimed at ensuring the security and prosperity of the state. For liberalism, the state was a necessary evil—which might not even be necessary. Liberalism took advantage of the growing importance of economics to the state, and of the state's inclination to 'draw back' from intervening, in order to ensure the 'free enterprise of individuals'. Out of this process there develops a notion of 'civil society' as something more or less opposed to, critical of, or a check upon, governmentality (see Danaher et al., 2000).

Foucault argues that the development of these two spheres— the interventionist, regulatory state and civil society—were not separate. The 'reason of state'—which promoted the existence, security and prosperity of the state as its end—produced the need for a civil society and a strong public sphere which would both criticise the effectiveness and necessity of the development of state policies of intervention and regulation, and in certain instances replace it. Questions of what constitutes moral or ethical behaviour, for instance, were largely removed in western democracies from the control of government, and became matters of 'public concern'. Think of the way in which, in contemporary western society, debates about contentious moral issues (euthanasia, homosexuality, promiscuity, abortion) are not so much driven by government policy but by 'pressure groups' (such as the various 'moral majority' groups in the US), who use the public sphere to push their positions and influence governments.

Traditionally in the West, the public sphere corresponded to a specific site or meeting place (a public square, for instance), where citizens could gather to discuss and debate their relation to the state and government. The public sphere was considered essential because it was meant to help citizens learn and make informed decisions about their society. With modern states it became impossible to gather citizens together in one place— although certain places are still used by the people when they want to protest against their governments. In the contemporary world the media has become the main site that links the public. Television and radio, for instance, are used to spread information, to represent points of view, to exchange ideas, to criticise policies, or to vent frustration or anger. This role of a substitute 'public sphere' has largely been seen, in the West, to have been taken on by non-commercial and non-aligned institutions such as the UK public broadcaster the BBC, but increasingly it has come to include all the media, especially the Internet.

THE STATE AND THE PUBLIC SPHERE

In many of Asia's most 'developed' states—the examples most often cited are Singapore, Taiwan and South Korea—there was, and still is, a close identification between political parties (and sometimes individual politicians) and the state. Moreover, the public sphere was not separated off from political apparatuses of the state. Quite the contrary, in many instances the state used the public sphere, particularly the print and electronic media, as a means of consolidating and extending its power, and censoring public opposition. More particularly, the public sphere, along with state bureaucracies (in important areas such as education, health and the military) were politicised in one form or another. The media were usually monopolised or regulated by the state, and played a central role in promoting the idea of the nation as a homogeneous and unified community. The most obvious examples of this occurred in communist countries such as China and North Korea, where the media were controlled by the Party. But in non-communist countries much the same happened, but usually less overtly. In India, for instance, the electronic media (in the form of the national television station Doordashan) was run by the state, while the print media were subjected to both legislative and informal means of control. Much the same was true of Indonesia under President Soeharto, and is still true of Malaysia, Singapore, Taiwan, China and Pakistan.

However, the 'domestication' of the public sphere may not always require any overt action by the state. In many postcolonised societies, the national intelligentsia itself has contributed to the formation of a 'domesticated' public sphere, bringing it in alignment with goals such as 'nation-building' (Srivastava, 1998). Some critics of postcoloniality have begun to argue that in many such societies, the elite have acted to impoverish the sphere of criticism and debate by too readily accepting that whatever the nation-state does is good for the society; by, in other words, reducing the life of the 'people' to that of the state.

India made extensive use of television in its attempt to promote a homogeneous version of the Indian people and nation. Doordashan, which was formed in 1959, primarily ran with education and news programs, but it also showed Hindi films and cultural programs. Doordashan promoted a notion of a largely Hindu and Hindi India, and tended to target elite upper- and middle-class audiences, favoured northern over southern India, and neglected and marginalised smaller ethnic groups and languages, such as Urdu and Assamese.

Indonesia attempted to make the same kind of use of the media, but in a much more overt way. President Sukarno wanted the media to function as a 'tool of revolution', while his successor, President Soeharto, described it as a 'tool of national struggle'. The values contained in the 'national ideology' of *Pancasila* served as a means of justifying tight control and regulation of all the media. Television, which was run by the state—generally by members of Soeharto's family—rarely allowed any disputation of the government line, and when it appeared likely that alternative opinions or views would be aired (in interviews with anti-government journalists or intellectuals, for example), they were quickly banned or censored.

THE PUBLIC SPHERE AND DISSENT

It would be wrong to conclude, however, that because governments closely regulate or monopolise the media, public spheres can't or don't function as sites for dissent, debate and the airing of alternative viewpoints. First of all the notion of the public sphere should not be confined to the mainstream media. The public will always attempt to find some kind of site or space in which to articulate opposition or criticism. For instance, during the post-Tiananmen crackdown by the Chinese government, dissidents had little or no access to television, radio or newspapers—such groups 'did not exist' as far as the state-controlled media were concerned. But they managed to get together for 'political' meetings and discussions at what conventionally were non-political sites and occasions, such as concerts, chess clubs, plays, art shows and other cultural events. In Indonesia and in other countries in Asia, cultural events (puppet shows, the performance of historical or traditional plays, comic acts) fulfil a similar 'alternative public sphere' function, as do more basic sites such as walls and noticeboards, not to mention obvious sites such as university campuses. In India this role is performed by a free press and a dynamic non-government organisation sector. Finally, in more affluent societies the Internet is increasingly becoming the most important site of 'public sphere' activity.

The media remains the most sought-after site, however, simply because it allows messages and information to reach the greatest number of people quickly. Because of this, dissidents have attempted to find ways of using the media without drawing too much attention to the fact—a situation which, in some ways, has been useful to both governments and opposition groups. Any attempt to completely edit out or close off alternative opinions or criticism (as is the case in North Korea and Burma, for example) has three major disadvantages. Firstly, it's almost impossible to do—as we mentioned earlier, people will always find somewhere to meet and speak. Secondly, a continuous refusal to allow the expression of any kind of dissent inevitably 'increases the political heat', which can lead to violent anti-government explosions (think of the speed and violence with which the Ceauşescu regime was overthrown in Romania, or the fall of Soeharto in Indonesia). Finally, a total (and violent) repression of dissent invariably attracts international approbrium, which can have concrete negative effects (for instance, Indonesia and Burma have been denied US financial and military aid for violently repressing opposition groups).

One of the ways that governments have dealt with this dilemma (how to monopolise meanings and ideas without seeming to deny the possibility of a public sphere) is to unofficially tolerate alternative viewpoints and even criticism, as long as they are covert and non-confrontational. A good example of this is the way the Singapore government seems to maintain a tight rein on public sphere activities, particularly in the media, while at the same time allowing covert expressions of alternative views in places such as arts performances and universities. For instance, the government would never allow anyone to openly promote, or take part in a discussion about, the merits of an 'undesirable' behaviour or lifestyle such as homosexuality. However, academics can produce 'scientific' papers about the effectiveness of AIDS pamphlets, or linguistic analyses of homosexual texts and discourses.

The very act of discussing or analysing such matters in a supposedly neutral way can be seen as a contribution—albeit a regulated one—to the public sphere, simply because it manages to provide an outlet for the dissemination of alternative information, and, in a *defacto* way, helps put certain issues 'on the agenda'. An example of this practice can be found in Ping-hui Lao's description of the growth, in Taiwan in the last decade, of what amounted to a 'critical public sphere' in the 'literary supplement' section of major newspapers—even those papers controlled by government interests or supporters. He writes:

These supplements stood out by devoting six to eight pages to cover such themes as new humanities, new space for public debate, new public opinion, and book or film reviews. The expanded weekend version continues to grow in Taiwan's major newspapers, although not in *Independence Morning Post*, in part because of the 1994 takeover of the newspaper by a millionaire KMT member of the legislature. However the *Post* now has daily cultural criticism columns written by a limited group of critics, and the subjects are always on media, gender, identity politics, etc (quoted in Wilson and Dissanayake, 1996: 341).

A result of these columns and essays has been the emergence of:

... several politicially significant topics in the public sphere ... not only in the streets where demonstrators gather on a weekly basis to speak about their identities, interests, and needs, but also in these cultural criticism columns where rational–critical discourse interacts with the events of everyday life. By appropriating the Chinese–Western tradition of writing intimate essays and turning the tradition into a cultural critique from within ... bilingual intellectuals have written 'to the moment' ... so that their readers can participate in the public sphere without losing sight of the international public sphere (341–2).

And on a less formal level, he points to the creation of:

... radio and cable TV stations for people to call in and comment. TNT, Voices of the Taiwanese, TVBS, and others draw a great number of cab drivers, opposition party members, housewives, and the working class to form a proletarian public sphere which is far more vital and mobile than the bourgeois literary public (346).

Similar uses of popular culture as sites of 'acts of resistance' to government control and censorship can be found throughout Asia—often by opposition groups reclaiming or contesting official 'national histories'. Chinese cultural critic Rey Chow writes that in many examples of contemporary Chinese popular music for instance:

... the question about popular cultural form is not a question of its ultimate autonomy from the official culture—since that official culture is omnipresent—but how, against the single audible decibel level amplified at random with guns and tanks, popular music strikes its notes of difference. The words of one of [the musician] Cui Jian's most popular songs, 'Rock and Roll on the Road of the New Long March', allude to one of the founding heroic events of the Chinese communist state, the Long March to Yanan. The last few lines go as follows:

What should I say, What should I do, in order to be the real
   me
How should I play, how should I sing, in order to feel great
I walk and think of snowy mountains and grasslands
I walk and sing to Chairman Mao
Oh! one, two, three, four, five, six, seven.

There is, first of all, the difference between the 'decadence' of the music, and the 'seriousness' of the subject matter to which the music alludes. Without knowing the 'language' we can dance to Cui Jian's songs as we would to any rock-and-roll tune; once we pay attention to the words, we are in the solemn presence of history, with its insistence on emotional meaning and depth. This is why Cui Jian's music so antagonized the officials in the Chinese state bureaucracy that he was dismissed from his post in the Beijing Symphony Orchestra and prohibited from performing in Beijing a couple of years ago . . . The official Chinese repudiation of his music is moralistic, aiming to reinforce a kind of obligatory cultural memory in which the founding deeds of communist ancestors are properly honoured instead of being played with—least of all through music imported from the capitalist west (Chow, 1993a: 387–8).

Up to this point we have concentrated on providing an account of how the public sphere operates, even when the state more or less monopolises or closely regulates conventional sites such as the electronic and print media. However state sovereignty is being increasingly challenged by the processes associated with globalisation, and this has ramifications in terms of the state's ability both to monopolise or regulate the media, and to delimit and control the activities of the public sphere.

THE GLOBAL MEDIA

Globalisation has produced three major trends with regard to the media. Firstly, there has been a push by western states, and international organisations such as the International Monetary Fund, to 'open up' media markets to worldwide competition. Secondly, there has been a massive concentration, in the last decade, of the media and communications market—usually corporations from the US, the European Union and, in some cases, Japan. Thirdly, there has been a process of corporations with different media interests and strengths merging to form super corporations (Time-Warner is an example), or of corporations taking over or entering into arrangements with a diverse range of media corporations (News Corporation is perhaps the outstanding example).

Either way the result is that a relatively small number of corporations now have fingers in most of the global media pies. In book publishing, for example, the top ten corporations (such as Bertelsmann, AOL-Times-Warner, and Viacom) control a disproportionately high percentage of the global market. In the film sector, the market is largely controlled by Disney, Universal, MGM, AOL-Times-Warner, News, Polygram, Pearson and Viacom, with only the Indian and Hong Kong industries offering much opposition to American domination. The main print news services are all European or American (AP, UPI, AFP), while Time-Warner's CNN satellite news service now reaches over 200 countries. And the top 40 advertisng agencies in the world are all from either the European Union, the US or Japan (Castells, 1998).

In the face of this kind of pressure, it is becoming difficult for Asian states to maintain their monopoly over, or regulation of, the media and the public sphere. In India, for instance, Doordashan has lost viewers to the privately owned Zee TV, whose programs are also run on the STAR satellite channel and which has the potential to reach Indian audiences both 'at home' and throughout Malaysia, Singapore, the Gulf States and in North America. Most of Asia, including China, can now access STAR, which is attempting to diversify its offerings in order to capture wider audiences across Asia.

While European or American corporations dominate global media and communications markets, they have increasingly sought to gain greater access to Asia. Perhaps the biggest obstacle facing Rupert Murdoch, and other global media operators who are currently attempting to carve up Asian media space, is the extraordinary heterogeneity of Asia. This can be seen in Table 1, which shows the population of each country in Asia set against three simple socioeconomic indicators: the proportion of people to telephones and televisions—good markers of the level of access that people have to information—and a somewhat more artificial indicator of economic success, the amount, per person in the population, of the Gross Domestic Product (GDP), measured in US dollars.

The higher the GDP the more economically successful the country is considered to be—but, it should be stressed, these indicators are very much a western construct, and should not be interpreted as measures of success in cultural 'civilisation' or social 'development'. A country with a high *per capita* GDP is not a 'better' country, or a more 'civilised' one than one with a low GDP. All such measures are contingent, as we are aiming to demonstrate in this book.

India's huge television audience, for example, is culturally diverse (along the lines of ethnicity, religion and class), and speaks sixteen languages and several hundred dialects. Local media operators (that is, operating at a national level, such as Zee TV, or at state and even municipal levels) are likely to remain competitive simply because STAR and other satellite operators can't adequately service (or afford to service) such a diversity of cultures and languages.

At the same time this culturally, politically and economically diverse Asia is the fastest growing media market in the world. Studies indicate that by 2005 television ownership will increase by 50 per cent in India, 33 per cent in China, and 25 per cent in Thailand and Malaysia. China alone could have as many as 800 million television viewers—which will stimulate competition for the chance to advertise to the new Chinese middle class. It is estimated that by 2005 the Asian advertising market will be worth US$20 billion (Castells, 1998).

Table 1   Contemporary Asia: telephones, televisions and *per capita* GDP

Country	Population	People per telephone	People per television	Per Capita GDP $US
Bangladesh	130 million	380	143.2	1040
Bhutan	800 000	96.9	175.4`	1570
Brunei	300 000	3.8	3.1	20 100
Cambodia	10.9 million	450	115.5	1350
China	1.2687 billion	17.9	3.7	3860
Hong Kong	6.8 million	1.5	3.0	23 105
India	989.2 million	53.8	16.4	1760
Indonesia	207.7 million	37	6.8	3275
Japan	126.5 million	1.5	1.6	22 720
Laos	5.3 million	181.5	101	1325
Macau	400 000	2.5	3.6	17 500
Malaysia	22.7 million	5.1	4.7	10 680
Mongolia	2.5 million	26.7	17.3	2315
Myanmar	48.8 million	217.3	147.1	1200
Nepal	23.4 million	120.5	185.2	1100
Pakistan	136.8 million	51	41.3	1660
Philippines	74.7 million	34.4	7.9	3475
Singapore	4.0 million	2.0	2.6	28 565
South Korea	46.9 million	2.1	3.0	12 995
Sri Lanka	19.0 million	36.1	12.0	2625
Taiwan	22.0 million	1.9	3.1	17 495
Thailand	62.1 million	12.6	4.4	6285
Vietnam	79.4 million	48.2	6.1	1755
(USA	273.3 million	1.3	1.2	31 469)

Source: *Asiaweek* 29 October 1999

CONCLUSION

For most Asian states satellite television represents, along with the Internet, the single biggest threat to their ability to regulate the public sphere—and thus the biggest threat to state sovereignty. However STAR has not had things all its own way in Asia. Rupert Murdoch was forced to drop the BBC World

Service News from STAR in order to appease the Chinese government, and in 1997 a warrant was issued for his arrest after STAR screened a program in which one of the hosts made derogatory remarks about Mahatma Gandhi. Furthermore, STAR's 'soft-porn' programs, usually screened late at night, have run into trouble from religious groups. In many respects, the idea that the globalisation of the media means a 'free market' of ideas is quite erroneous. In India, for example, STAR news presentations operate according to an elaborately formulated set of guidelines, intended to take account of Indian 'national' interests. This may include a restriction, or ban, on reporting on 'secessionary' movements.

Regardless of just how effective STAR, CNN and ESPN are in penetrating markets in Asia, however, the wide availability of satellite and cable channels effectively signals the end of state control of the public sphere in many countries in Asia—a situation which will be exacerbated once more people get access to computer technology and the Internet. What the states do have up their sleeve is the ability to intervene to make things difficult for media operators. With a variety of se-cessionary movements also contributing to Asian nation-states' sense of loss of authority—and which also utilise new media technologies to achieve their ends—this may come to be regarded as a necessary step for 'national security'.

In many parts of Asia the ability of states to monopolise the media and control the public sphere may be, in most cases, a thing of the past, but governments as diverse as those of China and Singapore will continue to regulate the public sphere in the interests of 'national unity and stability'. However there is little doubt that the forces of globalisation are likely to both exacerbate various nationalist 'discontents' throughout Asia, and contribute to a speeding up of the transformation of tradi-tional sites of identity politics such as religion, gender and ethnicity. In our next three chapters we will look at how the relations between global forces and cultural politics are being played out in those three areas.

SUGGESTIONS FOR FURTHER READING

Castells, Manuel (1998) *End of Millennium*, Blackwell, Oxford

Hall, Stuart (ed.) (1997) *Representation: Cultural Representation and Signifying Practices*, Sage, London, in the *Culture, Media and Identities* series

Hall, Stuart and Paul du Gay (eds) (1996) *Questions of Cultural Identity*, Sage, London

Hall, Stuart and Don Hubert (eds) (1996) *Modernity: An Introduction to Modern Societies*, Blackwell, Oxford

Lim, Shirley Geok-Lin, Larry E. Smith and Wimal Dissanayake (eds) (1999) *Transnational Asia Pacific: Gender, Culture and the Public Sphere*, University of Illinois Press, Champaign

6

Religion

This chapter does not aim to provide a 'comprehensive' picture of the religious milieu in different societies in Asia. Rather, our aim is to offer an introduction to some themes which we think are important in thinking about religion in Asia. Along the way, we will depart from conventional analysis by suggesting that, in addition to its role as a belief system, the religious sphere may also be a site for the playing out of a range of processes and events that characterise modernity in Asia. This is not to suggest that religion is a mask for other (say, economic) interests. Rather, in the contemporary world 'the religious' cannot be meaningfully separated from a range of other human processes, activities and desires.

The view that 'Asians' posit no separation between religion and society is one which is also part of the critique of perceived Eurocentric bias in the study of societies in Asia. In other words, it is argued that to make such a separation is to impose European categories, or ways of thinking, upon the study of societies in Asia. To adhere to this perspective in a dogmatic fashion, however, means accepting the idea of an 'authentic' native perspective, quite removed from the centuries of contact between cultures (between the western and the non-western as well as between non-western ones). It is an attempt to return to the now discredited notion of the self-contained anthropological village, untainted by contact with the outside world, and able to reproduce its worldview through reference to its own, unchanging, traditions. At this point in the history of the human world—in the aftermath of colonialism, and in the midst of advanced capitalism and globalisation—it is meaningless to adopt a position that fails to take account of different modernities in Asia and the processes of change and adaptation they have wrought upon different societies.

Central to much western theorising about societies in Asia is the supposed fundamental influence of religion upon the everyday conduct of 'Asians'. What really differentiates Europeans from non-western peoples, the argument often goes, is the lack of differentiation between religious and secular life in some societies in Asia, and the separation of the two spheres in European life. Western films such as *A Passage to India*, *A Year in Tibet* and *The Year of Living Dangerously*, which supposedly seek to represent the 'essence' of 'eastern' life to westerners, suggest that there is an unbreakable bond between 'Asians' and their religious beliefs, a bond without which 'we' cannot 'properly' understand their societies. American society, on the other hand, is very rarely represented (for instance, in travel advertising) as 'deeply' religious. And yet, public demonstrations of religious belief—such as professional football players praying together before and after a game, or media coverage of the president's worship in this or that church—would appear to belie the popular belief in the secularisation of American society. Indeed, presidential addresses to the nation always conclude with the sentence 'God bless America'.

Notwithstanding this, however, it is primarily some societies in Asia and elsewhere which continue to be viewed as 'fundamentally' religious. In part, though perhaps most importantly, the reasons for this lie in the recent history of European perceptions of the 'east'. Specifically, this attitude, as we saw earlier, marks the intersection of two related processes: colonialism and the discourses of European identity that emerged from the Enlightenment. The colonial era provided Europeans with the most sustained opportunity for developing and elaborating classificatory systems through which the categories of 'us' (Europeans) and 'them' (Asians, Africans, etc.) were established. There were several ingredients to this classificatory schema, and typically these included: male/female, adult/child, rational/irrational, this worldly/other wordly, and history/myth.

Such classifications have several effects. They reduce all

aspects of 'Asian' existence to some unbreakable bond with unchanging religious beliefs so that all motives, desires and actions come to be seen as being driven by, and derived from, the master narrative of religion. Further, religious beliefs and practices in some societies in Asia also often come to be characterised as fixed and directly traceable to an original point thousands of years ago, rather than as the consequences of complex interactions between processes such as colonialism, the struggle for power between different groups (rich and poor, men and women), the imperatives of 'nation-building' in the postcolonial period, electoral politics, and the current impact of the processes of globalisation.

RELIGION AND THE STATE

In tandem with pressures exerted on religious beliefs and practices by the forces of modernisation, capitalism and globalisation, religions—both 'official' and 'local'—have been forced to 'bend with the wind' and remake themselves. The interconnection between various Buddhist 'movements' and the states in which they are predominantly located constitutes a particularly good example of how the relationship between religion and the state is negotiated in contemporary Asia.

Buddhism was founded by Gautama Siddhartha (c.566–486 BCE). A Kshatriya by caste, Gautama is reputed to have left his home at the age of 29 and taken to the life of a wanderer in search of spiritual enlightenment. He is said to have achieved this state in 531 BCE in the town of Bodh Gaya, located in the present-day state of Bihar in eastern India. Upon achieving the state of enlightenment, Gautama came to be known as the Buddha ('the awakened one'). A considerable part of Gautama Buddha's early teaching consisted of pointed critiques of Hindu orthodoxies, such as the caste system. This won him some influential converts who helped to make Buddhism a major religious force, not just in the Indian region but also, through the work of missionaries, in many other parts of Asia.

It would appear that for much of its period of activity in India, Buddhism was dependent on the patronage of kings and others with substantial resources to support it. With the decline of such patronage, Buddhism, too, declined as a religious force, and by the tenth century it flourished more in other parts of Asia than in the land of its origin.

In our present time, what is important to remember is that Buddhism across Asia encompasses a wide assortment of practices, rather than being a monolithic 'essential' tradition. As well, like other 'Asian' religions, the varieties of Buddhist traditions in Asia have developed through a process of longstanding historical interaction between Mahayana (the Great Vehicle) school and the earlier Hinayana school. During the ancient period, adherents of both movements seemed to have coexisted peacefully, while disputing the validity of each other's scriptual sources. The Mahayana version became the dominant one in China, Japan, Korea, Mongolia and Tibet, whereas Sri Lanka became the firmest foothold of the Hinayana school (also referred to as Theravada Buddhism). A third movement within Buddhism, designated Vajrayana (the Thunderbolt Vehicle) occurred around the fifth century of the common era. There is a consensus among contemporary scholars that the distinctions between the three schools is not as easily made as earlier assumed, and that there are many overlaps in terms of practices and scriptual sources.

All of these movements came under considerable pressure from the state and the forces of modernity after the Second World War. Steinberg et al. write, for instance, that Theravada Buddhism:

> has been greatly affected by the nature of the regimes under which it existed during the 1960s, 1970s, and 1980s. Buddhists in urban Thailand were drawn away from strenuous adherence by the strong pulls of 'modernization'; fewer and fewer young men felt obliged to become monks, even for a short time, while the number of men choosing to remain monks for longer periods has declined even more sharply. In Laos and Cambodia, Buddhists found religion closely monitored by socialist regimes, but in Burma and Thailand, monks gifted at preaching, healing, and giving advice, as well as hermits renowned for ascetic practices, attracted large followings, and some monks in Bangkok curried favor with the new conservative middle class by vehemently attacking the 'devilish' character of communism. Theravada Buddhism enjoyed a revival in Burma after

independence, encouraged by official and unofficial state support, and there were in particular renewed forms of private practice, such as meditation, which became increasingly important to the urban devout. Although Burmese found it difficult to invest money in manufacturing or agriculture, religious edifices . . . have been given vast sums of gold, silver, and money by the laity (1987: 464–5).

The process of contestation between religions and the state sometimes takes quite overt and even 'confrontational' forms. Generally, however, state 'coercion' of religion is handled 'bureaucratically'. Steinberg et al. explain that Buddhism in Vietnam in the 1980s was no longer seen by the state:

> as a single spectrum of higher and lower traditions, both of which may be involved in peasant life; instead, it was divided into two categories, one tolerated while the other was not. As part of its conciliatory but managerial approach to the Buddhism of more urbane, educated people, the regime . . . opened a High Level School of Vietnamese Buddhist studies. The government, however, is hostile to manifestations of popular Buddhist millenarianism, even those which are wholly nonpolitical. Soothsayers, sorceresses, and shamans who under traditional dynasties (and the French) might have been watched but not forcibly converted to other occupations are now condemned not just for being potentially subversive but for being 'backward'—obstacles to a more scientific, economically rational culture (1987: 465).

When this 'bureaucratic' approach fails, more direct means are often used. In July 1999 the Chinese government banned the Falun Gong spiritual movement, further clamping down on the organisers in December 1999 by giving long prison sentences to the group's leaders. This was widely interpreted as official fear of a civil society organisation which was growing so rapidly, and in such committed ways, that it was seen to be a potential threat to the power of the ruling Communist Party. It was not simply a clash of ideologies—of alternative voices existing in mutual respect of each other. The extent to which so many people in China were joining the millions worldwide who were already part of the group, and committing themselves to its ideals, clearly shocked the government into repressive action, despite the repeated assertions by Falun Gong leaders that they had no political ambitions.

Over 35 000 followers of the Falun Gong movement in China have been detained since the July 1999 ban because, according to the government, 'the cult' obstructed justice, caused human deaths and illegally obtained state secrets. But the harshest sentences were given to those in the movement who were Communist Party members (including members of the ruling Politburo) as a strong signal for others to come back into line. The Chinese government read this movement as a 'cult' practising anti-state activities, whereas its own members see it as a spiritual movement combining meditation exercises and ideas from Taoism, Buddhism and from the founder of Falun Gong, Li Hongzhi. Its aims, the movement states, are to promote good health and good citizenship, but the issue for the Chinese government is where the line is to be drawn between religion, spirituality and social and political activism.

'CHINESE RELIGIONS'

Irrespective of the national context, it is generally true that the religious sphere in many societies in Asia has been characterised, for a very long period of time, by a multiplicity of influences. What many in the West currently understand as 'Chinese religions' or 'Indian beliefs' are the results of long and complex periods of interactions—not always non-conflictual—between a range of beliefs and practices involving other human endeavours and identities. It would be impossible, then, to speak of an 'original' Chinese or Indian religious system without also taking into account the interactions between Confucianism, Daoism and Buddhism in the former case, and the long history of coexistence of Hindus and Muslims within shared spaces in the latter.

With regard to China, for instance, scholars identify at least four different traditions: popular religion, Daoism, Buddhism and Confucianism. Perhaps the simplest way of thinking about the differences between the popular religion and the other three is to think of the former as non-institutionalised practice, and the latter as organised around, among other things, scriptural and other philosophical codes, clergy and formal allegiances to the organisation of devotees. Further, the modes of transmission of popular religion are more varied than that of the other traditions, involving visual, performative and oral traditions. The beliefs and practices that fall under this rubric are shared by a wide cross-section of Chinese people, both (in recent times) within China and Taiwan, and among diasporic Chinese populations around the world. Further, it is important to remember that Chinese religious practice—the everyday engagement with the divinity—displays a great deal of overlap between the so-called popular and the institutional religions. The various gods, spirits, cults, malevolent and benign ancestors, and deities of Chinese religious life are in a constant process of transmigration from supposedly differentiated religious realms, and present themselves in different forms according to the adaptive strategies of Daoism, Buddhism, Confucianism, and popular religion.

An important characteristic of Chinese gods is their representation as members of bureaucracy, sharing features of territorial jurisdiction, hierarchy, adherence to prescribed rules of behaviour and differentiated functions in common with their earthly counterparts. The bureaucratic terms in which Chinese heavens and gods are represented are echoed, some scholars suggest, in the manner of communication between mortals and deities. Hence, just as in this world, where the written word forms an indispensable part of any bureaucracy, scriptural offerings and their ritual burning form an important part of the communication process between the human supplicant and the supernatural being. The prevalence of the bureaucratic imagery in the sphere of the divine may have resulted from the great power of the institutions of the state in various aspect of Chinese life, resulting in an attribution to the heavens of those forms of power which seemed most real, and most overwhelming, on earth.

One of the most popular perceptions of the 'traditional' Chinese religious cosmos among westerners concerns the notion of bipolarity in nature, commonly expressed through the terms *yin* and *yang*. Indeed this 'bipolar worldview' (Thompson, 1974: 4) has become a very common aspect of western popular culture and 'new age' movements, being widely represented through personal items of jewellery and art.

It is estimated that the *yin–yang* theory of the material universe came to be established sometime between the fifth and the third centuries BCE. The English biologist and historian Joseph Needham has provided a historical 'reading' of the theory of the 'two fundamental forces':

> Some facts about Yin and Yang are . . . clear. We know, for instance, that the Chinese characters for Yin and Yang are connected with darkness and light. Yin involves graphs for hills (shadows) and clouds, and the Yang character has slanting sun rays or a flag fluttering in the sunshine . . . These correspond well with the way in which the terms are used, for example, in the Shing Ching (Book of Odes), a collection of ancient folksongs. Here Yin evokes the idea of cold and cloud, of rain, of femaleness, of that which is inside, dark like the underground chambers where ice is kept for summer use. Yang, on the other hand, evokes the idea of sunshine and warmth, of spring and summer months, of maleness and brightness. Yin and Yang also have more factual meanings: Yin the shady side of a mountain or valley, Yang the sunny side (Ronan & Needham, 1980: 160).

Along with *yin–yang*, *dao* is the other important aspect of ancient Chinese religion. The principal of *dao* is often understood as the fundamental reality that encompasses all appearance or, in some versions, as the laws of nature that constitute the essence of surface appearance. The connection between *yin–yang* and *dao* is that the material reality of the former is itself reliant on the (natural law) processes of the latter. It will be noted in all this that we have not had much to say about the nature of a supreme being in Chinese religion, as would be the case in a discussion of, say, Christianity. The most obvious reason for this is that such a figure may not be part of the Chinese cosmology, and to search for a supreme being 'behind' the cosmological principles of *yin–yang* and *dao* may only serve to reduce Chinese religious beliefs to terms familiar to the West. Instead, supernatural powers tended to be attributed to a host of deities and heavenly bodies. It is this worldview that finds play (and its narrative content) in the extremely popular Chinese ghost-story genre of Hong Kong films. In these films the other-world is occupied by both friendly and malevolent spirits who impinge upon and influence the living and their worldly affairs. The practice of ancestor worship—the act of propitiating the spirit of departed kin—falls within this framework of religious belief.

There are two general points that need to be made about Chinese religious beliefs. Firstly, Chinese religions are predominantly anti-humanist, which means that human beings are merely one aspect of the overall scheme of the universe, rather than being positioned at its centre—an outlook quite foreign to the Judaeo-Christian tradition. Secondy, our discussion of 'Chinese religion' does not mean to suggest that there existed a 'purely Chinese' body of belief the origins of which can be traced to an unchanging 'ancient' lineage. In fact Chinese religious belief was constituted through a wide range of influences including the 'folk traditions' of animism and naturalism, Buddhism, which came from India, as well as the 'local' canons of Confucianism.

This hybridity of Chinese religious belief has counterparts in other aspects of our understanding of Chinese societies. Western notions of the immutable 'traditions' of Chinese society, such as the supposed centrality of filial piety, are often contradicted by the more complex picture that emerges through a focus upon the diversity of beliefs. Recent scholarship points out, for example, that there exist several deities whose actions are at odds with both the patriarchal strictures of being a 'good wife', and filial piety. For instance, certain female deities refuse to marry and have sons, and escape the strictures of looking after aged parents by committing suicide. In these ways, the supernatural world may, in some instances, provide a critique of the structures and orders of society which may embody, for example, various forms of gender oppression.

During the modern period, the dynamic nature of some Chinese religious beliefs (by which we mean a diversity of doctrines) should also be seen as part of the constant 'reinvention' of Chinese culture which the nation-state has sought to define through its own vocabulary. At the local level—families, villages, and regions—we find a constant process of contestation between the centralising efforts of the nation-state, and the attempts to create new meanings. Our inability to account for this process of change, one scholar has argued, is due to the models of analysis employed: '[The] application of Western models of elite political struggle has made it difficult to see the central role of the contestation and reinvention of "Chinese culture" by local cultural forces . . . to nationalising and modernising efforts at many levels and in many parts of China' (Dean, 1998: 157). Interestingly, in this context (and in the broader context of state intervention in local lives, and globalisation), there appears to be a resurgence of regional cultural practices in some parts of China:

> In the irrigated Putian plains in Fujian province, the average village has six temples, each housing on average fifteen deities. Something like forty-five days of ritual perform-ances take place on an average in each village every year. Some villages hold over 250 days of theatre and ritual a year. Children in rural Putian have now reached adolescence in a world marked increasingly by temple festivals and ritual performance of cultural difference (Dean, 1998: 166).

An important influence upon the resurgence of local religious traditions lies in the input of Taiwanese and other Chinese communities around the world, who have provided financial and other support for a range of rituals, festivals and pilgrimage circuits. The input of Chinese diasporic communities (and diasporic communities in general) upon their 'home' culture is a complex and important area of study. So, Dean (1998) points out that the so-called 'conferences of the gods' organised around major cults in China, and enthusiastically supported by various diasporic Chinese communities, have played an important role in the dialogue between 'local', national and emerging global cultures as seen, for example, in the Hong Kong magazine pictured in Figure 10, where Chinese horoscopes are sandwiched between western horoscopes and an article on the pagan festival of Halloween.

Further, all this must itself be placed in the context of 'the commercialisation of Chinese television, the commodification of culture, the transformation of pilgrimage into cash-crop tourism, and the expanding impact of homogenised international post-modern capitalist culture (best exemplified by the Karaoke craze sweeping across China)' (Dean, 1998: 179). While we should not romanticise the ability (or the motives) of local communities in contesting centralising and globalising tendencies, these processes may nevertheless tell us something about the ability of religious beliefs and practices to offer resistance—and to create

Figure 10   East is sandwiched between West in this Hong Kong weekly

new forms—in the face of the larger, homogenising, processes. The most important aspect with respect to religious belief is its changing nature. In fact, it may be suggested that a theory of change is implicit in Chinese religious belief systems in the sense that within them 'the cosmos itself is constructed and subject to change, along with the individual, and . . . the changing set of perspectives on a changing cosmos can never be encompassed in a single system' (Dean, 1998: 167).

HINDUISM

The contemporary sense of the terms 'Hinduism' and 'Hindu' appears to have its origins in the seventeenth century. Prior to this, these terms were mainly used to refer to the inhabitants of the regions that extended beyond the river Indus (in present-day Pakistan). In their present sense, then, the history of these terms owes something to the history of western scholarship on India, the power of colonialism to impose its categories of thought, and the strategies of anti-colonial and nationalist movements that sought to define an Indian identity (and Indian/Hindu achievements) as both accommodation of and resistance to colonial rule.

The scriptural model of Hinduism, which presents the ideals of the Hindu religious world, is intimately concerned with the fourfold *varna* system that divided society into four hierarchically ordered groupings. The four *varnas* consist of the Brahmans or religious specialists, the Kshatriyas or the kings and warriors, the Vasyas or the trading classes, and the lowest in this hierarchy, the shudra, whose duty it is to perform tasks that the above groups do not perform, and who must also serve the latter in various ways. The term 'caste' does not itself correspond to the *varna* system, and the most common Indian referent of caste is *jati*. The gradation and the relationship between *jatis* is far more fluid than might be implied by the *varna* system; however, all *jatis* are able to locate themselves within the former. In a sense *varnas* are the ideal–typical descriptions of the Hindu religious world, whereas *jatis* constitute the reality. A multitude of *jatis* exist within each *varna* category, with 'demarcation' disputes at their borders, as well as disputes about these borders themselves. *Jatis* themselves may differentiate into several sub-*jatis*, each adopting means of differentiation such as endogamy (marriages within the group), or minute differences in procedures of ritual performance.

An important aspect of caste in the postcolonial period has been its mobilisation in the cause of electoral politics such that conglomerations of *jatis* have come to form substantial 'vote banks', and constitute a major part of the election strategy of political parties in India. We elaborate below on some of the characteristics of the Hindu caste system (for it has also found its way into non-Hindu communities). However, it is important to remember that we are not describing a static system, and that caste-related practices vary in their form depending on contexts such as social class, regional location, the actions of the state, the influence of the forces of globalisation, the nature of interaction in urban environments, and so on.

A key aspect of the caste system, and one which differentiates it from class, is its closed nature: all Hindus are born into a caste and cannot, as individuals, move out of their caste. However, it is possible over time for a caste as a collective to move up (or down) the hierarchy of castes. The sociologist M.N. Srinivas coined the term *Sanskritisation* (Srinivas, 1962) for one of the processes through which a caste may move 'up'. So, for example, the 'upper' caste of Kayasthas had, in nineteenth-century Bengal, a much lower ranking than other castes, but 'moved up' by adopting the characteristics of higher castes, and through accumulating educational 'capital'. It is also important to keep in mind that while the *varna* system has validity on an all-India basis, *jatis* may not correspond across different regions, with the lack of correspondence being particularly sharp between north and south India (and particularly in the 'middle' areas of the hierarchical chain, characterised by claims and counter-claims about relative position).

Another important aspect of caste is the distinction between purity and pollution, a distinction that underlies the principle of interaction and distance, in terms of status, between castes. So, Brahmans are ranked as occupying the highest point on the purity scale, with other castes following in descending order. Groups that fall outside the caste system, those without caste, as it were, pose an absolute threat of pollution through association to members of caste society; whereas within it, the threat of pollution varies with relative ranking. However, the causes of pollution are not merely other humans, but also elements such as bodily wastes; hence, the upper castes seek to preserve their purity through limiting their contact with such material and allocating tasks such as disposing of it to the 'untouchables'. In some instances, women may also prove a source of pollution for men, and should be avoided during, say, times of menstruation. In general, and in keeping with the masculinist ideology within castes, post-pubescent women are perceived to present a constant threat of pollution to men. These attitudes carry more or less weight depending on contemporary social and cultural circumstances.

What might be called the geography of caste is still a relevant fact of life in many non-urban environments in India, as well as in those localities of the city where the social and economic life of the village is, in some ways, reproduced; for instance, in poor localities and slum clusters. The most common pattern of residence in multi-caste villages is one of physical distance, and different caste groups tend to live in separate clusters of houses. This pattern may be repeated in urban slums where the pattern of migration is often determined by both regional and kin factors. In other, 'urban' parts of the city, such conglomerations are, of course, difficult to maintain. The act of sharing food, or rather, eating together, (commensality) is another important aspect of the traditional caste system, and in contexts where caste values still hold sway, the taboo against commensality is still quite strong. And not only are there strictures against co-dining, but the rules of pollution also prohibit, in many village contexts, 'low caste' people from drawing water from 'upper caste' wells.

In recent times, political mobilisation among non-upper caste groups has often been organised around resisting and changing such practices. Again, we must emphasise, our discussion cannot account for the reality of a changing situation; in an urban environment, for example, caste identities may be far more difficult (though not impossible) to ascertain, and restaurant dining, means permitting, does not allow for segregation along caste lines.

The theory of castes is also based on the idea of occupational specialisation such that, in principle, the kind of work a person may do is dependent upon caste membership; so the caste of leather-workers, carpenters, cattle-herders, dairy farmers, etc. follow occupations passed down the family line. However, as scholars point out, while it is true that such division of labour did equate to reality, even in the past it was never completely determined by its ideological underpinnings.

The doctrine of *karma*—the idea that a person's present life is dependent upon deeds committed in previous lives—also forms an important aspect of Hindu religious belief. The cycle of births and deaths in which humans are caught up—and they may do better or worse in each life depending upon the store of their good or bad deeds in past lives—may be escaped, however, through the act of renouncing the attractions and lures of material and emotional ties. In western literature and films, the Hindu renouncer is often refigured as the 'holy man', eschewing familial obligations and attachments with an 'other-worldly' bearing in pursuit of *moksha*, deliverance from the human cycle of birth and death. However, the 'other-worldliness' of the renouncer has often come to be interpreted as a characteristic of Hindus in general, whereas it is only a very specialised aspect of the belief system.

It has been noted that 'myths of Devil, the great Goddess, constitute a "hegemonic narrative" of Hindu culture' (Kakar, 1990: 135). Indeed, the Hindu pantheon includes some extremely powerful representations of the female form, none more so, perhaps, than the personifications of *shakti* ('power'), the goddesses Durga and Kali. However, notwithstanding this, religious texts ascribe a firmly subservient position to women. Representations of femininity in the Hindu world oscillate between the debilitating restrictions of the goddess and the whore. Women, as we have noted above, are more polluting than men, and classical texts direct men to keep firm control over 'their' women. The longing for a male child in Indian society is, in part, linked to the religious valorisation of men over women.

In recent times, media reports have made readers familiar with a custom which was thought to have been banished during the colonial period. The practice of *sati*, or widow immolation, is seen to derive its force from the belief that a woman's rightful place, in life and in death, is beside her husband. However, it is not clear that the reasons for some of the contemporary instances of *sati* can simply be laid at the door of 'religious belief', and there is considerable debate over the matter.

Moreover, there are several exceptions to the rule of women's subservience. Older women, for example, enjoy considerable authority within the household, and women's autonomy is much greater in non-upper caste contexts where the ideologies of ideal Hindu femininity do not hold great sway.

It is important to keep in mind that there has been considerable scholarly debate about *different* types of 'Hinduisms', in particular, whether there are 'upper' and 'lower' types of Hinduism adhered to by Hindus located at different levels of society. The version we have outlined above is traditionally referred to as the Brahmanical one and, although it provides an important frame of reference, there are other systems of belief within Hinduism that provide alternative frameworks. We should be wary of viewing Hinduism as a monolithic religion with a centrally organised belief system. 'Hindu beliefs' constitute a diversity of quite disparate ideas and practices, some of which, as in the cult of *tantrism*, reverse all that is considered sacred in 'mainstream' Hinduism. Some 'Hindu' practices may appear quite alien to many Hindus themselves.

What is true of Hinduism, however, is the profusion of divinities embodying almost every conceivable characteristic perceived by humans, as well as supra-human ones: there are divinities personifying wealth, diseases, knowledge, creation, destruction, regeneration, agricultural prosperity, mechanical dexterity, rain, sun, death, speed, good luck, husband-worship, ideal femininity and the virgin. The orientalist stereotype of a polytheistic religion with over 300 million gods and goddesses, though extreme as all stereotypes are, carries some empirical validity. As well, many of the gods are 'human' in their peculiarities and predilections: there are those that overeat, love sensuous pleasures, express uncontainable anger and violence, selfishness and vengefulness, and generally disregard the 'godly' virtues that are the hallmarks of divinity in the Judaeo-Christian tradition. The Christian distinction between 'good' and 'evil' is rather more difficult to transpose upon the Hindu world, in which divinities may take on 'good' and 'bad' characteristics in different contexts. Further, forms of divinity may be either pan-Indian or 'local', that is, worshipped at the level of the family, the clan, the village or the region.

No system of belief, however, can ever be completely extracted from the history of the society of which it is a part.

And it is important to remember that Hindu beliefs and practices have been subject to criticism from within their own ranks and, in some cases, such criticism has led to the emergence of new belief systems. These include Jainism, founded by Vardhamana (*c.* 599–527BCE), and Buddhism.

Further, various aspects of contemporary Hindu identity—at least those connected with 'upper caste' Hinduism—have their roots in a variety of colonial and nationalist processes. So, if orientalist scholarship unified Hinduism and described it through a study of its 'holy books', then nationalists went along with this and even more vigorously relied on certain religious texts to form the cornerstone of Hindu beliefs and practices. In effect, as recent scholarship has argued, the British colonisers and their opponents, the nationalists, 'collaborated' in producing a view of Hinduism that was monolithic, homogenising, unchanging, and, through being text-centred, one that marginalised practice.

Many of the current 'central' texts of Hinduism took on this status only during the colonial period. The most significant reasons for this are twofold: European scholars (such as the German Max Mueller) brought to orientalist scholarship the biases of western textualist traditions of the study of religion; and Indian nationalists sought credibility for their cause through securing validation from such scholarship. If Christian missionaries and their supporters argued that colonialism had a 'civilising mission', then Indians could point to the great tradition of Indian learning as embodied in the religious texts such as the *Vedas*, and to a 'golden age' of Indian civilisation that once purportedly existed. In time, the 'great texts' became identified as the 'authentic' form of Hinduism, and all practices that departed from their prescriptions were viewed as aberrations.

The colonial period also saw an important development connected to the great goddess theme we mentioned earlier. During the late colonial period in India, the most dominant nationalist thinking on the nation-to-be represented it as a virtuous woman—most commonly through the notion of a revered mother. In some versions this was achieved through representing India as a Hindu goddess. The rationale for the choice of the mother figure lies in the fact that there also exist 'uncontrollable' goddesses within the Hindu pantheon, and hence it became important for a masculinist nationalist ideology to choose images that leant towards 'domestic' aspects of the divine feminine. Further, as feminists have pointed out, the women = goddess = India formula also led to the identification of women as 'Indian tradition' itself, and 'purity', 'fidelity' and 'piety' came to be identified as the 'essential' virtues of Indian womanhood. Any departures from this in real life were seen to be an insult to the idea of the nation. Hence, in this way, colonial and nationalist processes combined to produce an idea of India as a Hindu entity and an idea of women that severely restricted their roles as human beings. In the postcolonial period, the most dominant visual representations of the Indian nation continue to be in the form of a virtuous woman as goddess.

In recent times, the term 'Hindutva' ('Hinduness') has been used by many Indians to signify the emergence of a 'proud' and confident modern Hindu identity, and by others to mark the rise of Hindu 'fundamentalism' antagonistic towards Muslim communities in India. Some scholars have suggested that the publicly professed (and constitutionally enshrined) religious secularism of the Indian state has also been accompanied by a concurrent, and implicit, Hindu framework of national life. So, for example, the Indian nationalist movement in its various phases explicitly employed Hindu themes and symbols in its struggles and, more problematically, often posited Islam as one of the enemies of 'Indian civilisation', thereby constituting the latter as essentially Hindu. The syncretic nature of the Indian life tended to be effaced in favour of sharply differentiated religious identities. In a sense, then, the present carries the legacy of these early political and cultural developments.

In our time, perhaps the most publicly devastating example of the construction of Muslims as the 'enemies within' is the destruction of the Babri Mosque by Hindu zealots in the north Indian city of Ayodhya in 1992. The medieval era mosque had been reputedly built on the site of a temple razed to the ground by a Muslim emperor, and the crowds that demolished it were seeking, it was asserted by their supporters, to avenge this historical slight upon Hinduism. However, notwithstanding the current popular wisdom, assiduously propagated by many Hindu organisations, that constitutes Hindus and Muslims as 'naturally' hostile communities for millennia, historical and contemporary evidence suggests otherwise. While we would not suggest a utopia of Hindu–Muslim relations in India, colonial practices that constituted Hindus and Muslims as enemies, and those of Indian nationalism that perpetuated such constructions, are certainly implicated in the processes of the present.

There is one further context that is of importance in understanding contemporary Hinduism. There has been since the beginning of this century organised resistance to the caste structure by those at the bottom of the hierarchy, for example, the Dalit (downtrodden) movement. Many anti-upper caste movements have coalesced around the idea that the discriminations suffered by the lower castes must be overturned. Legislative responses by the state have included job reservations for members of disadvantaged communities, and the provision of 'reserved' electoral constituencies to ensure representation from previously disenfranchised groups. Many lower caste groups have also chosen conversion to other religions (primarily Buddhism, Islam and Christianity) as a way of countering the ignominy of their position in Hindu society. However, despite the various changes in the caste system over the past 50 years or so, it is still correct to say that in most non-urban areas the lower castes continue to face discriminatory practices, and that instances of inter-caste interaction in the urban areas continue to be confined to the upper castes.

ISLAM

In more parts of Asia where Islam is a major presence, an important aspect of the understanding of the various contexts of the contemporary situation lies in comprehending the context of the colonial encounter. This is as true of the countries of Southeast Asia, as it is of those in South Asia. The colonial situation—including European interpretations and indigenous responses, and various policies which also had consequences for the religious sphere—served to produce a postcolonial present within which it is impossible to speak of a 'pure' Islamic tradition that has existed unchanged for centuries. We will provide examples that illustrate this colonial 'angle'. Finally, as we have emphasised with regard to various other contexts, Islamic 'traditions' are in a process of constant flux, influenced by those very contemporary processes that are responsible for many other changes in the lives of people in Asia.

There is some consensus that Islam was first introduced to Southeast Asia between the thirteenth and fourteenth centuries by Arab and Indian traders. However, conversions in any substantial numbers first occurred during the fifteenth and sixteenth centuries, and the clearest context of these conversions appears to have been those of trade and cultural interaction. For many reasons, Southeast Asian Islam has not, until recently, received serious scholarly attention. One of these is linked to a perspective developed during the Dutch colonial period in Indonesia. It has been suggested that colonial scholars and administrators collaborated to produce a perspective on Indonesia that regarded Islamic influences as merely shallow accretions upon 'deeper' and more long-lasting non-Islamic traditions; and that the 'true' nature of the people could, in fact, be 'best' understood by concentrating on non-Islamic religious traditions and upon pre-Islamic past.

In the field of law, for instance, the colonial period saw the emergence of a colonial legal system that distinguished between 'customary' law that, it was asserted, may or may not accord with 'Islamic' law. Recent critique has suggested that this gesture tended to be repeated by many influential scholars of Indonesian society in more recent times. Over the last three decades of the twentieth century, anthropologists and historians vigorously disputed the premises of this position, and we now have a picture of Southeast Asian societies that does not proceed through the propagation of essentialised notions of identity.

At present there are approximately 200 million Muslims in the regions of Southeast Asia, with the majority belonging to the 'orthodox' Sunni sect of Islam. Islam in Southeast Asia exists in two kinds of national contexts: in nation-states where Muslims are a majority, such as Indonesia and Malaysia, and in countries where they form a minority, such as the Philippines, Singapore and Thailand. Consequently, 'Islamic issues' in the two different contexts—the majority and the minority—are often quite different in nature. The most obvious of these differences is that in the Muslim-majority states the struggle for recognition of 'Islamic values' as part of the national mainstream does not face the same obstacles as it might in the 'minority areas'. And, in some instances in the latter societies, as in the case of Mindanao in the Philippines, struggles for regional autonomy often take on the form of a conflict between the majority and the minority religions.

However, scholars also note a difference in the manner of the articulation of Islamic concerns even within the Muslim-majority states. So, in the case of Malaysia, it has been suggested that the fairly even split in numbers between Muslims and non-Muslims, and the state's emphasis on 'ethnic solidarity', has given rise to a more conservative Islamic ideology than has been the case for Indonesia. Here, the colonial context is also important. In Indonesia, the Dutch colonial regime was much more confrontationist towards Islam than was the case in Malaysia, where the British were content to leave it under the authority of local elites. In turn there developed within the Indonesian Islamic milieu a tradition of critical debate and discussion that appears to have been absent in the Malaysian case (Muzaffar, 1988).

The role of Islam in anti-colonial struggles in Indonesia was a prominent one, and the struggle itself was considerably influenced by symbols and justifications drawn from the Islamic world. However, after the mid-1960s, Islamic political expressions tended to be largely proscribed by the military government that then came to power after a bloody suppression of the communist movement. In the subsequent period, the chief public manifestations of religion allowed were of a 'cultural' nature, with Islamic bodies involved in a variety of social welfare and 'reform' activities. Strict control was exercised over perceived political acts by Islamic organisations and their leaders but this has now been loosened, and Islamic political organisations play a largely unfettered and influential part in Indonesian politics, as the election of the Islamic candidate Abdurrahaman Wahid to the presidency in 1999 testifies.

In Malaysia, perhaps as a consequence of the control exercised by local elites over religion during the colonial period—through the agency of the British colonialists—there has always existed during the postcolonial period a more established relationship between the state and Islamic bodies, hence the tensions between the 'civil society' of Islamic organisations and the organs of the state that surface from time to time are nowhere near as strongly articulated in Malaysia as they are in Indonesia. An important aspect of the renewed interest in the study of Islam in Southeast Asia is linked to what is commonly referred to as the 'Islamic resurgence', or revival, in the region. Broadly put, this refers to the demand for an incorporation of the values and principles contained in the Koran and the *Sunnah* (the Prophet Mohammad's way of life) into the legal, political, administrative and cultural spheres of the state. The revival—with the 1970s and the 1980s marking its advent—involves a wide cross-section of the Muslim population, and its meaning varies according to regional context. It has been suggested that, in many instances, the western media have tended to focus on the more sensational aspects of the revival (such as the demand for certain forms of punishment for criminals) which may, in fact, not have the support of many sections of society. Indeed, there are many instances when 'Islamic revival' tends to be represented as a 'return to the past', rather than as an attempt by some to think about the future.

An important aspect of the so-called Islamic revival in Southeast Asia is its orientation towards the concerns of a population often situated within various contexts of modernity, and seeking to engage with tensions between secular and religious life in late capitalism. It is not, in other words, a debate about strictly theological issues being conducted among religious specialists. In the Southeast Asian context, the demand for the institution of Islamic values in public life constitutes the demand for a negotiated place for Islam in modern governance, rather than a complete 'Islamicisation' of the state itself. Hence, while this position rejects the idea that religion and state should constitute separate spheres, it also accepts that many aspects of modern statehood require a variety of organisational principles.

One way of viewing this situation is to think of it as an attempt to re-examine western models of growth, development, and society. There are many thinkers contributing to this process, including those from South Asia and the Middle East, whose writings contribute to a growing body of literature and debate that is popular among a wide cross-section of (though, it should be said, mainly urban) populations in Southeast Asia. Finally, it is important to remember that the banner of 'Islamic values' may sometimes be indistinguishable from the straightforward quest for political power in the context of electoral politics. This is to say that the goals and principles of Islamic politics have both influenced, as well as been influenced by, the processes of modern nation-states. This, of course, is quite similar to the case of other major world religions.

The other major area with a concentration of Muslim populations is South Asia. There are approximately 300 million Muslims in the countries of South Asia and, in global terms, only Indonesia has a larger Muslim population than India. Pakistan and Bangladesh are Muslim-majority states. Muslims constitute approximately 11 per cent of the Indian population, with Sunnis outnumbering Shiites in South Asia in general. There are substantial cultural overlaps between the peoples of Bangladesh and those of the state of West Bengal in India. There are reports of Muslim settlements during the seventh century, but the first substantial Islamic presence in South Asia came about during the eighth century. By the eleventh century it had established itself as a major political and religious force, with a variety of 'ethnic' groups, including Turks, Afghans and the descendants of the Mongols, contributing to a historical process that has produced a complex and syncretic culture. The Mughal empire, established during the sixteenth century and nominally existent until the nineteenth, is considered the most important of the Islamic kingships in South Asia.

Islam came to South Asia through a succession of time periods and hence its impact does not display a singular set of characteristics. For this reason, it displays different characteristics in different parts of the region, influenced by the different sets of local customs with which it interacted and by the guiding themes of the different periods of history within which it established itself. Islam's history in South Asia displays a characteristic that is also true of other parts of Asia: Islamic beliefs and practices have been as diverse as the cultures among which they have been implanted. Islam's spread across the world has not, in other words, produced a homogeneous Muslim identity.

In a manner similar to that described for Hinduism, both the Muslim leadership and the colonial administrators in South Asia sought to portray Islam as a monolithic, unchanging and unified religion. Each had their own reasons for doing this. So, the various distinctions of class, region, language and even 'caste' tended to be elided in favour of a homogeneous identity. These representations received a fillip during the colonial period from such moves as the creation of separate electorates for Muslims (the so-called Morley-Minto Reforms of 1909), which served to further the notion of a distinct Muslim identity, one left untouched by the centuries of inter-action between different communities in the subcontinent. And yet, across India, Muslims in different regions speak different languages, and often practice different customs: hence Muslims from the eastern state of Bihar are likely to have more in common with local non-Muslims than with Muslims from, say, the south Indian state of Kerala, or from those from the northern states of Punjab and Kashmir.

Across Asia, too, Muslims differ from each other in quite salient ways. For example, the caste system of the Hindus is also a part of the social structure of the Muslims of Nepal, Pakistan and many parts of India whereas, quite clearly, this is not the case for those living in, say, Indonesia or Malaysia. However, while there may exist a caste system among certain Muslim communities, it also differs in several ways from the Hindu caste system. So, for example, among Pakistani Muslims from the Punjab region, notions of ritual purity and pollution are not important determinants of caste, as is the case among Hindus.

It is important to remember that we seek to make a distinc-tion between religious ideology (which, in the case of Islam, is one of equality of all Muslims) and practices generated by the history of Islam in different parts of Asia. It has been reported that the caste structure tends to get reproduced among immi-grant South Asian communities such as those in Manchester in England. The primary purpose of caste for Pakistani Muslims in a diasporic environment appears to be linked to the arrangement of marriage alliances.

In contexts where Muslims constitute a minority (though a very substantial one), there is another peculiarity that may be absent in those societies in Asia where Muslims are in the majority. Research from India suggests that ideas of religious boundaries are far more complicated than might be suggested by notions of Muslim identity. Specifically, it has been suggested that many Hindus at the lower ranges of the caste hierarchy share many more cultural features with Muslims than they do with Hindus from the higher castes. Indeed, there is much research to suggest that it may be more meaningful in many instances to speak of a shared composite culture of groups living in proximity to each other, rather than attempt to discover sharply delineated religious identities.

RELIGION AND GLOBALISATION

We have emphasised so far the importance of the processes of globalisation in the study of religious spheres in Asia, and would like to conclude this chapter by reiterating its significance. Two specific examples will suffice. In recent times, the diasporic Indian community (particularly in the US and the UK) has proven to be an important source of support for the Hindu fundamentalist movement in India, providing both financial and moral support. The new technologies of communication have been important in this process, with, for example, the Internet being used to constitute a worldwide network for disseminating information and gathering support.

The events surrounding the publication of author Salman Rushdie's *The Satanic Verses* also tell us something about the articulation of the global process and the religious sphere. The responses to Rushdie's book, although they occurred in a variety of different contexts, gained their impact from the increasingly intermeshed nature of the global sphere. So, Muslims in Bradford in England protested against it, the Indian government placed a ban on it and the Iranian government issued a *fatwa* in Rushdie's name: all events that gained wide coverage through the communication between immigrant Muslim communities in the West and through the global media itself. The end result was an 'event' the public nature of which owes substantially to the various aspects of globalisation. It may be in the diasporic situation that the idea of a singular Muslim identity stretching across the globe comes to be most strongly established. Among other things, this is also an aspect of the search for 'heritage' undertaken by many diasporic populations who feel marginalised from the life of their host communities, and turn towards explorations and assertion of identity politics that may not, in fact, have much resonance in their countries of origin.

CONCLUSION

It is important to remember, however, that while this chapter has provided an outline of some of the major religious traditions in Asia, we have not been able to do full justice to the actual religious diversity in the continent. We have not, for instance, provided coverage of Sikhism (founded in the sixteenth century by Guru Nanak in north India), Christianity (a major presence in many parts of Asia), Buddhism, Zoroastrianism (whose followers are known as Parsees, and who first arrived in India during the tenth century), Hindus in Bali, and a variety of other sects and cults (including animists) which have substantial followings and distinctive histories. We can only urge the reader to keep in mind this diversity and to remember that the enumeration of 'major' religious traditions does not exhaust the variety of belief systems in Asia.

At the beginning of this chapter we made the point that religion was one of the sites which have been used, in the West and elsewhere, as evidence of an eternal, unchanging 'Asian character'. Much the same is true with regard to notions of gender and gender relations. In our next chapter we will look at the relation between gender, sexuality and identity politics in contemporary Asia.

SUGGESTIONS FOR FURTHER READING

Balibar, Etienne and Immanuel Wallerstein (1991) *Race, Nation, Class: Ambiguous Identities*, Verso, New York

Chow, Rey (1998) *Ethics after Idealism: Theory, Culture, Ethnicity, Reading*, Indiana University Press, Bloomington

Feuchtwang, S. (1992) *The Imperial Metaphor: Popular Religion in China*, Routledge, London

Hasan, M. (ed.) (1998) *Islam, Communities and the Nation: Muslim Identities in South Asia and Beyond*, Manohar, New Delhi

Hooker, M.B. (1998) *Islam in South-East Asia*, E.J. Brill, London

Shahar, M. and R.P. Weller (eds) (1996) *Unruly Gods: Divinity and Society in China*, University of Hawaii Press, Honolulu

7

Gender and sexuality

In this chapter we consider how gender and sexuality function, both historically and in contemporary contexts, as sites of the imposition, contestation and transformation of certain identities in Asia. Before we consider these issues, however, it is useful to clarify some terms, and introduce some of the main arguments, that have come out of recent debates about 'gender politics'. Firstly, it needs to be pointed out that what is understood by the terms 'man' and 'woman' is in no way universal or ahistorical. We might think that everyone knows what a 'man' is, but this usually means taking our own cultural and historical circumstances, ideas and values and presuming that they apply to other countries, cultures and times. As we make clear in this chapter, this is not the case: what is meant by 'masculinity' and 'femininity' (and the values they come to represent) is always being 'renegotiated' as circumstances change.

Women (in Asia and elsewhere) have been, and still are, discriminated against. But what has become known as 'patriarchy' manifests itself in a variety of ways, and can, and has been, resisted by women. It is important to look beyond seeing 'patriarchy' as something that has reduced all women (particularly Asian and 'third world' women) at all times to dupes and slaves of men, or as something that completely defines gender relations. As Judith Butler suggests: 'The very notion of "patriarchy" has threatened to become a universalizing concept that overrides or reduces distinct articulations of gender asymmetry in different cultural contexts' (Butler, 1990: 35). And of course the idea of

Asian women as being submissive and passive is one of the stereo-types that has informed western perceptions of Asia, most particularly with regard to 'orientalism'. As Edward Said writes:

> Flaubert's encounter with an Egyptian courtesan produced a widely influential model of the Oriental woman: she never spoke of herself, she never represented her emotions, presence, or history. He spoke for and represented her. He was foreign, comparatively wealthy, male, and these were historical facts of domination that allowed him not only to possess Kauchuk Hanem physically but to speak for her and tell his readers in what way she was 'typically Oriental' (Said, 1985: 6).

When we use the term 'patriarchy', then, we are referring, in a general way, to the institutionalised and systematic valuing of men over women (and the consequences of that discrimina-tion), and not to the inevitability or homogeneity of discriminatory gender relations.

The second issue we need to consider, closely related to our previous point, is that gender politics is always tied up with other considerations such as the history of, and changes to, the notion of 'masculinity' and, as a corollary, the politics of 'sexual preference'. It may seem a strange thing to say, but a 'man' is not always a 'man'; that is, what is meant by 'being male', or 'masculinity', varies from one culture to another (the same applies, of course, to the notion of 'woman'). There has been, of course, considerable ambiguity regarding western discourses on oriental men. On the one hand, films, novels and other cultural texts have often represented them as oversexed, rapacious 'animals', a variation on the 'bloodthirsty, sadistic animals' of *Blood Oath*, the Australian film about the Japanese that we discussed in Chapter 1.

And yet another side of orientalism has involved represent-ing oriental men as 'feminised', submissive, effeminate or sexually inadequate. In an episode of the animated series *South Park*, Japanese men plot to 'control' American children by way of the 'Pokémon' craze. When parents confront the Japanese businessmen and accuse them of threatening the US through cultural means, the Japanese dismiss the charge and allay the fears of the townspeople (or at least the fathers), by pointing out that all Japanese men have small penises, while American men have big penises—so they couldn't possibly be a threat to America.

The ironic nature of this discourse is, of course, not always understood by everyone and, indeed, similar ambiguities and inconsistencies characterise the way some Asian cultures 'gender' their own identities. In the Philippines, for example, some political leaders and aspirants try to outperform each other in displays of their sexual prowess and 'machismo'. For instance, while running for president, Juan Estrada played up his 'vices' (womanising, heavy drinking and partying) and was elected by a large majority of the (largely Catholic) voters. The same 'over-performance' of masculinity in Japan would not be tolerated by the electorate. And yet feminists in Japan have often expressed outrage at the way Japanese male politicians more or less openly keep mistresses, and engage in extramarital affairs; they point out that similar behaviour by women politicians would cause scandals, and end careers. The point is that whereas in the Philippines some politicians need to go over the top in performing their masculinity, in countries such as Japan, these masculinist tendencies and values are more or less recognised and valorised, but never flaunted.

These issues become even more complicated (and politicised) when we take sexual preference into account. When men and women engage in same-sex relationships, their 'status' is usually transformed into something that is often characterised as unhealthy, deviant, unnatural or perverted. In other words, they become 'something other' than 'normal' men or women, a process which is often accompanied by discrimination and/or criminalisation.

These and other issues play a significant part in the way identities—at the levels of nation, ethnicity, class and the individual—are 'played out' in many Asian contexts. In the remainder of this chapter we will provide some contexts for these issues, and exemplify how they inform contemporary practices.

WOMEN AND ASIAN CONTEXTS

The seeming paradox of societies in which there exist beliefs that strongly value women, while in everyday life a woman's lot is one of considerable hardship and discrimination, often strikes western (and, indeed, many Asian) observers as part of the 'irrationality' of Asian societies. However, the perception of a paradox may itself derive from perspectives that assume that societies in Asia, for example, can be comprehensively understood through a focus on what is considered to be a determining factor of 'Asian' lives, such as religion. For while it is true that most religious systems in Asia speak highly of women, it is also important to focus on the social practices through which cultural beliefs are played out in their everyday life. It is useful to look at these in terms of four interrelated issues:

- the history of the 'women's issue' in Asia
- the extent and types of women's disadvantage in contemporary societies in Asia
- the representations of women as part of a wider politics of gender, and
- the nature of initiatives taken by women of a wide variety of backgrounds towards resisting their marginalisation and towards offering alternative visions of a more equal society.

The latter is important to consider if we are not to subscribe to the perspective of monolithic 'non-western woman', who is unable to mount challenges to her situation, and must await intervention by men or western women. For, contrary to traditional representations of many societies in Asia in anthropological and historical literature, there exist examples of contexts where male dominance has never been complete, and where women have exercised considerable autonomy in the conduct of their lives. For instance, 'the structurally central role of Negeri Sembilan women', in Malaysia, 'especially as mothers, women's frequent involvement in kin decision-making, the importance of their position in households where a man moved to the woman's village on marriage, women's often extensive property rights and their ideological centrality' (Stivens, 1996: 3) suggests a more complex picture of Asian gender issues than is traditionally imagined.

There is one further aspect to keep in mind in terms of the present context. In as much as many people have come to see Asia as a relatively homogeneous cultural entity, it is a result of several centuries of western scholarship and practices of representation. Just as we should avoid the tendency to homogenise Asia, we should also remember that the situation of women in different societies in Asia can also differ markedly. The category 'third world woman', for example, is far too monolithic—that is, it presents a homogenised idea of non-western femininity—and far too generalised to capture the complexities of the situation in reality. The position of women and their participation in the 'public' life of their community in Asia does, in fact, vary greatly from country to country.

So, in South Asia, Sri Lankan women enjoy a higher quality of life, a higher literacy rate, as well as a higher participation rate in the workforce than their counterparts in, say, India and Bangladesh (Jahan, 1992: 5). The situation is different again in Southeast Asian countries, where indices such as literacy rates, workforce participation and health provide a more positive picture of gender equity when compared to those in South Asia. Again, while in some countries in Asia there is a declining female/male sex ratio due to various measures that affect the survival chances of girl-children and female foetuses, in other countries (such as Japan and South Korea) women's position in society has progressively improved through a combination of state action and non-governmental activism. Literacy rates for women in South Asia generally appear to be about half that of men (Jain et al., 1992: 8); however Sri Lanka is, again, the exception with a much smaller gap between female and male literacy. Compared to the other countries in South Asia, women in Sri Lanka are also better positioned in terms of life expectancy (around 67–70 years), representation in the primary and tertiary education sectors, and in the workforce. However, we should keep in mind that in all these contexts the indices for women's well-being are consistently lower than those for men.

THE HISTORICAL CONTEXT

During the colonial period in Asia, there were several movements concerned with women's rights. However, these can be more properly described as women's welfare rather than women's rights movements. Their main aim was to secure some degree of dignity for women, rather than absolute equality with men, which was perceived as a very distant goal. During the colonial period in India, both men and women (although there were more men 'reformers' than women) agitated in the areas of widow remarriage, the immolation of widows, child-marriages and in several other contexts where women were seen to be oppressed because of their gender.

However, some feminist historians have suggested that while, on the one hand, the agitation for women's welfare during the colonial period brought to light the issue of gender equality, its use of certain rallying points also tended to reinforce stereotypical ideas regarding women. The 'symbolic use of the mother as a rallying device' (Kumar, 1993: 2) may have had this effect. Some of the most prominent women activists during this period included Pandita Ramabai (1858–1922) who, among other activities, established a school for child-widows in the west Indian state of Maharashtra; Sarla Debi Ghosal (1872–1946) who was a strong advocate of revolutionary terrorism in Bengal in the cause of Indian nationalism; and the Irishwoman Annie Besant (1847–1933) who was the first woman president of the Indian National Congress, the political party that was to lead India to independence from the British.

A combination of concerns for female emancipation and nationalist goals were also present in those other parts of Asia which experienced colonial rule. So, in Indonesia the name of Raden Ajeng Kartini (1879–1904) continues to be invoked in the context of 'the history of the struggle of women for freedom from entrenched oppression' (Coté, 1992: ix). And, like many women of her time in other Asian contexts, Kartini, too, struggled 'with both the prescriptions of traditional life and the uncertainties of modern life' (Coté, 1992: ix).

Historically, the most active participation of women in public life in India was witnessed during the campaigns against British rule, and throughout the latter half of the nineteenth century an increasing number of women began in various ways to take part in activities other than those traditionally prescribed for them. This trend only strengthened during the twentieth century as nationalist movements around the country gained both in focus and organisation. In the period 1905–08, a time of considerable nationalist activity and upheaval in Bengal, 'middle-class nationalist women contributed jewellery as well as money [towards the movement]; [and] in some villages women began to put aside handfuls of grain as contribution' (Kumar, 1993: 41). An indispensable aspect of the encouragement given to women's causes during this era was the belief that an improvement in their conditions of life would lead to there being 'better' mothers, and hence 'better' offspring to people a rejuvenated nation. The concern for issues such as women's education and women's health was, in other words, a functional one, and it can be argued that it did not view women as the ultimate beneficiaries, but only as the means to an end: healthy and well-educated women would mean 'efficient' motherhood, which in turn would produce healthy workers and a 'robust' motherland.

Another aspect of historical interest is the connection that was made by several women's rights activists in India early in the twentieth century between greater rights for women and Hindu revivalism. That is, the issue was couched in terms of images and vocabulary borrowed from a Hindu worldview. More often than not the linkages made were quite explicit. So, often, women were represented as having the powers of certain Hindu goddesses, and the movement for women's rights itself was likened to a (Hindu) religious activity. In many ways this situation was a direct consequence of a colonial context where (Hindu) Indians perceived their religion to be under attack by Europeans, and considered it important to highlight its 'strengths'. Further, while an increasing number of women began to raise the 'women's issue' in public, their formulation of the debate was one where women's role in public life (and especially in the burgeoning nationalist movement) was seen to be an auxiliary one: they were to supplement the efforts of men rather than take up positions of leadership themselves. We will see below how this idea pops up, quite unexpectedly, in some of the ways the 'modern' Asian woman is represented in the contemporary period, especially in advertisements.

During the postcolonial period, women in India have taken part in a wide variety of political activities. These have ranged from the relatively conservative All India Women's Conference (founded in 1926), whose members mainly belonged to the well-off sections of society, to the communist-inspired movements for sharecroppers' rights, known as the Telengana movement (1948–50), and the revolutionay Naxalite movement of the 1960s and 1970s. Some important contemporary issues that have been taken up by various women's movements in India are: alcoholism and gambling by husbands, violence against women (often, but not always, as a consequence of alcoholism), rape, 'dowry deaths' (where the bride is killed, usually burnt, for bringing 'inadequate' dowry), price rises, educational opportunities for girls, attempts to control women's sexuality and police corruption. Of course, the extent to which these various movements have, either explicitly or implicitly, taken on anti-patriarchal positions has tended to vary depending upon factors such as the political affiliations of the movement leaders, and the background of the majority of the women themselves.

Historically, then, both women and men have been involved in the struggle for women's rights, however, the discourses and strategies of such activism, much feminist scholarship has pointed out, have not always been unproblematic. So, in many national movements in Asia, 'woman' functioned as an important sign in the masculinist constructions of the idea of the nation-to-be which came to be represented through the notion of the 'mother-who-is-the-nation' (Zutshi, 1993: 94).

THE CONTEMPORARY SITUATION

This chapter opened with an observation regarding an apparent paradox: the contradiction between the respect assigned to women in theory versus their actual situation. In many countries in Asia there have been (and are) a number of influential women political figures (past and present heads of state in Bangladesh, India, Pakistan, the Philippines and Sri Lanka, for example), as well as leaders of oppositional movements (in Indonesia, Malaysia and Myanmar). However, in all these societies, this appears to have made little difference in terms of women's rights, for 'none of the women leaders in South Asian countries where female leadership has strikingly predominated has concerned herself in any overt way with women's issues, and even less with women's movements' (Rajan, 1993: 105). How do we begin to understand this apparent paradox?

Firstly, we need to be careful not to make simple connections between the relatively high percentage of women leaders in Asia and the position of women in general. In fact, the attempt to analyse the context of the woman leader in Asia has posed considerable dilemmas for feminist scholars. The rise of a number of women to prominent positions of power in these societies has not necessarily meant the empowerment of women in general (as some streams of feminism may have predicted), and the woman leader has, in fact, merely adopted pre-existing modes of practising authority without any concern for a politics of 'sisterhood'.

Secondly, it is important to understand that the woman leader in Asia may not be significantly representative of Asian women in general; that is, she is the 'product' of quite a specific set of historical circumstances and, usually, comes from a stratum of society that may have few inclinations towards radical politics. Almost all the women leaders in Asia have tended to be drawn from the elite sections of society, and have had male relatives (father or husband) precede their political presence. Their acceptance as leaders in male-dominated societies may, then, be a complex consequence of the lingering adherence to legitimacy of dynastic succession, the popular perception of women as the guardians of 'family tradition', and the social and political importance of certain families in postcolonial societies.

Often these families (the Nehrus in India, the Sukarnos in Indonesia, the Aung Sangs in Burma, for example) were intimately involved in anti-colonial struggles that led to political independence for their societies, and have gained recognition as having made 'sacrifices' for the sake of the national community. As well, the established culture of masculinity also has a place for the idea of the woman as the mother-of-the-nation such that the woman leader comes to be represented as the nation itself ('Indira is India' was a popular slogan during Indira Gandhi's long reign as prime minister). The woman leader's position is seen as legitimate not because of her abilities to lead, but rather because of the supposed attributes of motherhood which, in turn, is presented as the incontrovertible destiny of all 'good' women. What this tells us, then, is not so much that the preponderance of woman leaders in Asia reflects the position of women in many societies in Asia, but that their emergence is linked to quite specific cultural and historical conditions.

The dominant role of the state in postcolonial societies has meant that women's movements in Asia have both relied upon it to provide equal rights for women, as well as having had to resist the forms of discrimination that the state itself has been instrumental in institutionalising (Rajan, 1993: 6). So, 'legislation has been a dominant and continuing demand of movements against women's oppression . . . [as] it has provided forms of escape and protection from existing social practices' (Kumar, 1993: 4). The higher quality of life enjoyed by Sri Lankan women can be directly linked to specific measures undertaken by the postcolonial state (Jayawardena, 1992). Feminist agendas in Asia may be seen to be quite different to that in the West. 'By liberation', Jahan points out, 'Asian women generally refer to women's access to better nutrition and health care, safe water and shelter, better education . . . etc' (1992: 6). And in many instances state intervention is crucial for such objectives, not least because of constitutional provisions that (in principle) guarantee the equality of all citizens. However, it should also be pointed out that women's movements in many countries in Asia have also existed in a state of considerable tension with the state's activities, for it has often been recognised that while legislative action may provide relief, it can sometimes come at the cost of increasing official intervention in the life of its citizenry.

An important context of the focus on women in a postcolonial situation is also the perceived contest between 'indigenous traditions' and 'foreign modernity'. We cannot emphasise enough the importance of this context for some situations in Asia in terms of legislative, political and cultural debates about women. Perhaps the simplest way of understanding this is to say that in many such debates women become the bearers of 'Asian tradition', and since traditions are generally seen to be fixed, the argument usually runs that in order to protect 'our' traditions from 'foreign' influence 'our' women must also be shielded from change. As discussed earlier, this was a common theme in colonial debates on women's issues. In many ways, then, debates about women (and quite often, carried out by women) in many societies in contemporary Asia can be best understood as the result of a complex series of alignments between historical processes (such as colonialism) and their absorption into contemporary dialogues about modernity.

One contemporary representation of women in Asia that exemplifies the modernity versus tradition debate concerns what some feminist writers have identified as the 'new woman'. Images of the new (or 'modern') woman can most often be found in the pages of glossy magazines which cater to the emerging and relatively prosperous urban middle and upper-middle classes, and in various forms of television texts such as advertisements and 'lifestyle' programs. The new woman is usually portrayed as 'attractive, educated, hard-working, and socially aware' (Rajan, 1993: 131), changing, as shown in the advertisement in Figure 11, 'with the times', like gold for 'the new Indian woman'.

Other important aspects of the representation are her independence, her career-mindedness and her ambitiousness. She is also, and perhaps this is the most important rationale for her presence in the media, a consumer: her income allows her to be an independent consumer, able to make her own choices. Hence she is an important source of commercial profit.

Figure 11   Pplatini advertisement, *Femina*,
February 1997

Feminists have pointed out, however, that it is inadequate to simply understand this model of contemporary womanhood in terms of the emergence of a new female identity in Asia. The representations of the new woman, it can be argued, are also in a way reformulating masculinist ideologies which domesticate political assertions for equality by women, as in the advertisement shown in Figure 12.

However, her 'newness' does not lie in putting forward an identity that is independent from her 'old' self, that is, one

Figure 12   Advertisement for Eagle Flask Industries,
Femina, 1 February 1997

Figure 13   Oral contraceptive advertisement, *Meri Saheli*, January 1999

within which her primary role is to be the self-sacrificing nurturer of the family. The advertisement in Figure 13 for a contraceptive pill is from a Hindi magazine aimed at women. It is particularly interesting in that it offers the choice of being 'modern' as part of the possibility of remaining 'traditional'. The statement attributed to the women in the advertisement is: 'I am mindful of all the needs of my family, no matter how small'. While sex is de-linked from reproduction (via the contraceptive pill) and pleasure is brought into the equation, at the same time, however, this notion is underplayed by linking female desire to the family—the woman's 'first responsibility' (in this case, the implied responsibility of not over-burdening family resources through another pregnancy). The new woman, as represented in Figure 14 may dream her own dreams, but only as long as these do not conflict with the needs of her family, engendering a broader context for the woman's 'primary' role in society.

An important aspect of these representations is the manner in which subtle (and sometimes not too subtle) codes that domesticate any hint of 'rebellion' are sutured into the image. 'Liberation' becomes an aspect of aspiring to marriage and domesticity, of having the welfare of one's family as the ultimate goal, of cherishing the heterosexual relationship, and of being a model consumer, always seeking and evaluating new products. The political struggles of feminism are, then, effectively represented as marginal to the project of women's rights, and the threats that feminism poses to the ideological structures of patriarchy are sought to be contained. Women's rights can be achieved, the representations of the new woman seem to suggest, without any questioning of established structures of control and oppression, whether these be those of patriarchy, capitalism, or any other forms of social discrimination.

In instances where public representations of middle-class women present them as independent economic subjects, there are additional problematic subtexts we need to keep in mind. So, for example, Krishna Sen points out that contemporary policy as well as consumer culture contexts in Indonesia favour representations of 'affluent working women' (Sen, 1998: 38), in contrast to earlier official positions where a woman was regarded as 'first a reproductive agent, then a faithful wife and mother, and an unpaid domestic worker and consumer' (Sen, 1998: 41). However, Sen goes on to say, while on the one hand

She respects tradition

She is open to change

New Woman

SHE'S A BIT LIKE YOU

Figure 14   Advertisement for *New Woman* magazine

such representations may be viewed as positive, on the other, they are also part of a process where the needs and rights of 'working class' women may become marginalised. Hence 'the politics of sex in contemporary Indonesia cannot be separated from the politics of class' (1998: 46).

In some instances, the new woman is also the bridge between 'modernity' and 'tradition'. She may be 'modern' but she is not 'western': that is, 'underneath' her confident modernity she retains the 'essential' values of her culture. So, for example, she respects her parents, and aspires to married domesticity. She is 'perennially and transcendentally wife, mother, and homemaker, [and] saves the project of modernization-without-westerniza-tion' (Rajan, 1993: 133). Here, the woman is part of a discourse of purity that has a long history in many societies in Asia. In the context of rapid change, this discourse is often utilised (by men) to maintain existing strictures of gender power through prescrib-ing certain types of 'approved' (or 'traditional') behaviours for women, as can be seen from Figure 15.

This is the cover of a cookbook (produced in 2000) from Hong Kong. Aimed specifically at the mothers of school-age children the book is explicit in laying the responsibility for their children's academic success on their own skill in the kitchen, with its cover emphasising retro male-oriented western imagery.

Figure 15   Hong Kong recipe book cover, 2000

Similarly, in China in recent times, there has been a marked shift in the representations of women in advertisements and other forms of popular culture such as magazine covers and 'calendar girl' depictions from the 'earlier defeminised images of the Mao era' (Hooper, 1998: 188). However, the reactions to these have come not only from critics of the objectification entailed in such representations, but also from various organs of the state with quite a different agenda. Hence, as one scholar has pointed out, 'in the face of the penetration of global capital and communication technology, the Chinese state is nonetheless attempting to fashion a new ('Confucianised') woman who is 'modern' and 'Chinese' but not 'western' in nature (McLaren, 1998: 196).

WOMEN AND CONTEMPORARY STRATEGIES OF EMPOWERMENT

While many people may think of the condition of most women in Asia as unequivocally and unrelentingly bleak, and their ability to offer resistance (unless 'assisted' by western feminist interventions of one sort or another) negligible, there is considerable evidence to the contrary. This evidence can be found in various spheres of activity. Notwithstanding the kinds of representations of Asian women discussed above (as 'modern' but subservient to male dictates, as seeking individuality but not necessarily equal political rights, and as uninterested in achieving equality through processes that may involve conflict), other models of women's subjectivity are also available.

For example, women's access to political processes—and not simply voting rights—is an important aspect of the struggle for gender equality. The activities of a women's group in an Indian village for example, provide an illustration of both the possibilities and the practices of feminist politics in Asia. As a consequence of long-term activism by the women's organisation Samagra Mahila Aghadi, 'a women's panel was elected to the *panchayat* (village governing body) in January 1990, and 125 women were given a share in their husbands' property' in Vitner village in the state of Maharashtra (Rajan 1993: 121). This instance of the participation of women in village-level politics presents us with a different model for thinking about women's empowerment than that linked to the context of 'prominent' women leaders. The feminist scholar and activist Gail Omvedt has pointed out that in Vitner the women elected to the village governing body have achieved 'local political power as part of a collective fight' (quoted in Rajan, 1993: 121), and that their numbers are drawn from traditionally subordinate classes and castes in Indian society.

In other parts of Asia, too, there are instances of women's engagements with processes and institutions that have tended to marginalise them. Many feminists may not necessarily classify all these activities as 'feminist' in as much as they may not fulfil the criterion of an explicit challenge to patriarchal authority in all its manifestations. However, as strategies of independence and self-esteem, it is important to see them as part of a broadly feminist endeavour that may also carry the potential for consequences other than those immediately imagined. The instances we will discuss below are drawn from contexts where international capital movements in search for greater profitability collaborate with national governments working in the name of 'development', laying waste the lives of the most vulnerable sections of society in their path. And, as we have already discussed, in the hierarchy of disadvantage, it is women who are at the bottom.

The relation of poor people and 'development' has tended to be one of forcible eviction, displacement, the razing of entire villages for commercial farming (such as Tambalar village on the island of Mindanao, destroyed in 1994 in order to construct a fishing port), and the flooding of villages for building dams (such as the Batangas Port Development project, about 100 kilometres south of Manila, financed by Japanese investment). The link between Japanese economic development and the misery of large numbers of people in other parts of Asia seems particularly salient. In many instances this has resulted from the commercialisation of agriculture, actively pursued by national governments in order to meet 'export demand', and the consequent dependence of local farmers upon multinational companies.

From around the mid-1980s, government-sponsored eucalyptus forestation in northeast Thailand through the privatisation of previously 'common' areas of village land has led to mono-culture but also to a serious diminution in the villagers' ability to generate a livelihood. Village lands have been appropriated by the government for commercial forestry, and as eucalyptus growth strongly inhibits other forms of flora, large tracts of land have been turned into 'eucalyptus deserts' (Matsui, 1999: 90–1). However, anti-eucalyptus plantation movements, with women at the forefront of negotiations with government officials, have ensured that the issue continues to be in the public limelight. Women have also been prominent in protesting against the construction of large dams that are seen to be destructive of the livelihood of a vast number of people, and whose objectives could be achieved by other means. In India, the agitation against the Narmada Dam project in western India is a case in point. The project once completed will cover an area of some 300 000 hectares of forest and 200 000 hectares of farmland. Financed by a variety of sources including the World Bank, the project has had a tumultuous passage due to the protests against it, protests in which women from various sections of Indian society have been active participants.

The formation of cooperatives led by women in the face of pressures of mega-development projects that threaten their already precarious existence are another example of the kinds of grassroots action through which many women in Asia have sought to offer resistance to such threats. So, projects such as the Balangon [banana] Growers' Association in Negros in the Philippines help to reconstitute community life in the face of massive displacement, as well as engendering a sense of confidence in an environment otherwise hostile to issues of gender equity. The PANMAI weaving cooperative (established in 1991) in Roeit province in northeast Thailand is another example of women's endeavour towards engaging with issues of gender politics through an intervention in the sphere of economic independence (Matsui, 1999: 143). For, as mentioned earlier, feminist analysis has identified economic independence as a cornerstone of a politics of emancipation. The founding of the Self Employed Women's Association (SEWA), an organisation of women working in marginal occupations such as 'vegetable vending, junk smithy, handcart pulling, trading in old garments, etc.' (Jain, et al., 1992: 10), in 1974 in Ahmedabad in western India was another step towards women's economic empowerment and political struggle.

Feminist magazines such as *Manushi* in India also provide an important forum for the furtherance of the struggle as well as avenues of sharing women's experience. There exists, in other words, a wide variety of processes and sites of grassroots women's movements in various parts of Asia, and though their existence has tended to remain relatively unrecorded (at least in the portrayal of Asia in the western media), their work continues to gather significant momentum, unfolding as it does on the borders of theory and practice.

Our discussion may lead some readers to conclude that many states in Asia have invariably been agents for the oppression of, rather than furthering, the aims of gender equity. However, we should be careful to avoid the somewhat simplistic tendency to essentialise the state through attributing to it an 'inherent "logic" of repression' (Frankel, 1983: 17). This, as Frankel suggests, is 'both misleading and politically dangerous' (1983: 17) for it only serves to make abstract the historically and culturally specific conditions of possibility of different state forms and their functioning. The state, in other words, is a site of contest rather than one of permanently fixed ideologies and interests. It is true that state neglect has largely characterised official attitudes towards 'women's issues', however, it is just as true that pressure from activists has also affected the focus and direction of official policies.

Hence, in India the colonial tendency that favoured secondary and tertiary education (Viswanathan, 1989) has tended to persist in the postcolonised period and there has been a phenomenal boom in these sectors. However, data for the same period show sharp declines in state-wide enrolment; that is, the numbers enrolling at primary, upper primary and higher secondary levels (in any one year) follow a markedly downward trend. It could be concluded that as students progress from grade to grade, for the vast majority of parents (or those in charge), schooling becomes a luxury, and only those whose education does not impinge upon the family's ability to earn a subsistence are able to continue with it. In the Indian case, female children, and those from 'scheduled caste' and 'schedule tribe' backgrounds would seem to be the first affected by the strategies of survival.

However, the case of China provides an important example of state action that has led to quite different results. Available evidence suggests that 'the adult literacy situation [in India and China] was very similar in the late 1940s. [And that] by

1981–82, there was virtually no difference between China and Kerala [the Indian state with the highest rates of literacy] for the younger age group, while India [as a whole] was left far behind'. (Drèze & Loh, 1995: 2872). Drèze and Loh point to the important role of the state in promoting educational activity in China, and as a consequence, the higher rates of female literacy in that country. Differential state action in China has meant that 'educational achievements are not only much lower in India than in China, they are also much less equitably distributed' (Drèze & Loh, 1995: 2870).

Even within countries in Asia one is witness to the impact upon social issues as a result of government action or inaction. One such example is the case of the south Indian state of Kerala. It has been suggested that Kerala has witnessed 'the growth of public politics and the fluctuation of women's roles' (Jeffrey, 1992) over the past 150 years or so, and that 'together, by the 1970s, they produced the attributes of Kerala that produced the epithet "model"'. During the above period, then, Kerala, a state poor in materialist terms, recorded the most remarkable achievements in terms of increased life expectancy of its inhabitants, decline in infant mortality and improvements in literacy figures in general and in female literacy in particular. These resulted, observers noted, 'in a perceptible difference to the quality of life' of the people (United Nations Report, quoted in Jeffrey, 1992: 6). While there are no simple answers to the achievements summarised by the term 'the Kerala model', we can, nevertheless, say something about the extent to which a politically active population, in which women enjoy some autonomy, may force governments to carry out programs that ease people's lives' (Jeffrey, 1992: 12). Some measure of the Keralan experience can be gauged by the fact that by the late 1950s, 87 per cent of primary-aged girls in Kerala were estimated to attend school (Jeffrey, 1992: 55). The role of the state in all this is most instructive and can be seen to offer hope for other models of governmental intervention in the area of gender equity.

MEN AND MASCULINITY

We made the point, at the beginning of this chapter, that 'a man was not necessarily a man': other factors (such as race, class, caste and sexual preference) often determine who were (and are) seen as 'real men'. Feminist and gender theorists such as Judith Butler and Leo Bersani have argued for the need to take a more relational and 'historicist' approach to the notions of masculinity and femininity. What this means is that the categories 'male' and 'female' are not 'natural'. Both categories have histories, and are subject to change. Moreover, the two categories are always understood, to some extent, in relation to one another. Feminists, for instance, have often argued that in contemporary societies the category 'male' constitutes the positive aspect of a binary (and is associated with 'virtues' such as strength and rationality), while 'female' is negative (and is associated with weakness and emotionality). More recently, some writers have argued that the binary is being reversed, and men are becoming 'the new women': this point is taken up later in this chapter.

The term 'gender', however, is still essentially deployed as a synonym for 'women'. In other words, while most theorists accept that the category 'woman' is culturally constructed, it is presumed by many that men just 'are'. But masculinity is not something that can be 'taken for granted': it 'is simultaneously a place in gender relations, the practices through which men and women engage that place in gender, and the effects of these practices in bodily experiences, personality and culture' (Connell, 1995: 71).

At any particular time there exist several models of masculine behaviour. As in our discussion of women in Asia, there are at least four contexts we need to consider in a discussion of masculinities in Asia. These are: the colonial era, the attempts by postcolonial nation-states to construct a 'modern' masculinity, the existence of indigenous trans-gender identities that, at least implicitly, contest dominant traditions of masculine behaviour and the effect of contemporary commodity cultures and globalisation.

The West's ideas about 'oriental men', for instance, have often been characterised by a racial 'devaluing'. As Edward Said writes, apropos of nineteenth-century attitudes: 'An Oriental man was first an Oriental and only second a man' (Said, 1985: 231). Clearly, an important aspect of the cultural politics of colonialism concerned the construction of gender identities of both the colonialists and the colonised. In many instances, the justification for colonial rule itself derived from adherence to codes of 'hyper-masculinity' that delineated 'proper' (or 'suitable') masculinity from 'improper' ones. So, 'native' males were characterised as not possessing the characteristics of European men that made the latter suitable as 'natural' rulers, while condemning the 'natives' to subjection.

Usually, the rationale for the inventory of 'manly' characteristics derived from Enlightenment discourses around the virtues of 'rationality', 'logicality', 'the scientific temper' and the ability to keep one's emotions in check. 'Natives', it was argued, lacked these characteristics and were, therefore, closer to women in their temperament. In this way, 'Asian' men tended to be feminised (with parallel implications about the supposed characteristics of women).

In some instances, the colonial rulers identified specific ethnic groups as possessing manly skills in such abundance that their entire being was defined by nothing more than such 'essential' manliness. However, they were also characterised as not quite the equal of the colonialists due to a supposed lack of intellectual qualities. Such groups—for example, the Gurkhas of Nepal, who continue to serve in a special regiment of the British army—came to be referred to as 'martial races'.

Nevertheless, the politics of masculinity has been an important aspect of the 'nation-building' projects of the postcolonial era. Postcolonial engagements with masculinity confronted colonial stereotypes of indigenous masculinity and, most typically, attempted to resist these through a simple inversion of the categories. So, nationalists now argued that 'Asians' (or rather, 'Asian' men) in fact possessed all those characteristics that were valorised by the colonisers. There emerged in the postcolonial era, then, the idea of scientific or 'epistemological masculinity' (see Srivastava, 1998) that sought to prepare the postcolonial citizen to be an equal of the white male. Such attempts also paid homage to colonial ideas about 'proper' manliness. The 'resistance' to colonial ideas ranged from the Chinese valorisation of the revolutionary soldier, the technician and the 'masculinised' woman (all imbued with 'scientific' method), to the abundant representations of engineers, scientists and doctors as heroes in Indian films. The latter have always had considerable intra-Asian currency, and the flow of such ideas across the countries of Southeast Asia has, since the 1950s, been a consistent one.

The contemporary era of economic and political liberalisation in Asia has its own bearings on the issues of sexualities and masculinities. Several anthropological studies have pointed to the existence of indigenous transgender categories in many societies in Asia (such as the *hijras* in India and the *kathoey* in Thailand) which, although not unambiguously accepted in 'mainstream' society, often have cultural sanction. The steady emergence of other non-heterosexual identities into the public sphere has been an important feature in many contemporary societies in Asia.

However, while some of these developments may serve to decentre established ideologies and models of masculinity, the same process can sometimes work to reinforce existing power relationships. The recent breakneck process of economic liberalisation in Vietnam has seen the emergence of sexual pleasure as a currency of exchange among potential business partners, with the sexual services of prostitutes being used to 'entertain' valuable commercial contacts, as well to seal business deals. In contemporary Vietnam, the sexual economy has become an important part of the free-market strategies of its entrepreneurial class that includes government functionaries.

An aspect of this is the 'commodification' of women's bodies. A male entrepreneurial class appears to be marking its upward mobility through reference to unhindered access to women's bodies, reinforcing heterosexual masculinity in the process, while women sex-workers suffer a denigration in their status. Further, the idea of 'traditional' Vietnamese masculinity also comes into play. The promotional strategies employed by the owners of many of the bars and hotels that provide sex sessions 'play up' the idea of a Vietnamese 'essence' embodied by their female employees. Typically, the women are transformed into 'native delights' that may be enjoyed by discerning Vietnamese connoisseurs, who, in turn, differentiate themselves from foreign businesspeople as well as establishing and expressing an 'essentially' Vietnamese masculinity (Nguyen-vo, 1997).

It might be expected that patriarchal attitudes would have broken down, at least in so-called 'developed' countries such as Japan, Taiwan and India, through exposure to the more 'liberal' attitudes of western modernity. But as Carole Pateman (Pateman, 1988) and other feminist theorists have pointed out, the Enlightenment, modernity and capitalism—the three major western 'gifts' to the rest of the world—have all perpetuated gender inequality in one form or another. The natural subject or identity of both the Enlightenment and modernity, represented and reinforced by figures as diverse as the French philosopher Rousseau and the Spanish painter Picasso, was male. And capitalism's major narrative, the romance, written up, filmed and photographed in any number of advertisements for cars, cigarettes and clothes, has invariably situated the male as the subject of desire, and the woman as his object.

This masculinism, and the gender relations it naturalises, have been taken up and reinforced—by politicians and state institutions—as an integral part of the well-being and 'health' of the nation. Figure 16 shows the cover of a brochure published by a 'sex clinic' in Delhi. It is aimed at men and women (though mostly men) from lower socioeconomic groups, and its audience mainly consists of recent rural migrants to the city, unskilled and semi-skilled industrial workers, and low-paid employees in the service sectors.

The messages encoded in this image are quite similar to those found in representations aimed at higher socioeconomic groups. These concern the 'normality' of the nuclear family, the dominant position of the male (or the father figure), the importance of the male child, and the desirability of westernised commodity culture. Further, it is also important to notice the quite specific representation of the wife-mother. She may be 'modern' (her hairstyle and the fact that she is happy to be part of the nuclear family), but 'underneath' it she is 'essentially' traditional: she wears a modernised version of the Indian sari, so she is not so modern as to seek complete equality with the male, either through adopting ambiguously western attire, or through occupying the central place in the illustration herself. She is modernity-without-westernisation personified, and obtains her fullest potential in that role; not for her, the image seems to suggest, the political struggles of an 'irrelevant' feminism.

These 'middle-class' discourses now find their way into non-middle-class ones through the greater access to media programs available to a very large number of relatively poor people; a general diffusion of a commodity culture of which sexuality has become part; and an emerging discourse on the public sphere. By the latter we mean the images of public parks, gardens, picnic grounds, tourist sites, fast food outlets, etc., around which discourses of Asian modernity are often gathered. For most

Figure 16   Front cover of the Ashok Clinic's brochure

young people from poor backgrounds, the only private spaces available to them are really public ones such as the parks and gardens in many urban centres. Here, various long-established fantasies of modernity (the desire for romance as seen in Asian and American films, for example) are played out. There is, in other words, an emerging culture of modernity in Asia to which a far greater number of people than ever before have access, and which is influential in the formation of contemporary gendered identities in Asia.

151

GENDER AND MODERNITY

We made the point earlier that the emergence of a culture of modernity was no guarantee of gender equality. As Carole Pateman (Pateman, 1988) points out, western modernity has in a sense done away with 'classical patriarchy', only to replace it with 'fraternity'; in other words, it has merely replaced one form of institutionalised inequality ('the rule of the father') with another ('the rule of brothers'). At the same time it is clear that modernity, like gender categories and relations, is not ahistorical or unchanging. The rise, in the West, of the feminist movement in the 1960s, which helped produce greater educational access for women as well as their entry into professions that were once exclusively male domains, or male-dominated (law, medicine, academe, engineering, business), has transformed gender categories and relations, and western modernity itself. If we want evidence of this, we only need to look to the numerous articles (appearing in newspapers and magazines throughout the West) warning that men are losing 'the battle of the sexes'. Consider the following sentiments articulated in an article, written by Dylan Jones, titled 'Are men the new women?'

> Everywhere you look these days we see the complete feminisation of all men. All types of cars are now designed for women, as are shops . . . drinks . . . bars . . . films, cinemas, bookstores . . . even sex shops. Anything that one might have once considered to be a male domain has now been subsumed by women. Caveman, it seems, has now turned into quiche man (Jones, 2000: 20).

Jones's comments, although ridiculously exaggerated, do pick up on two important, related points. Firstly, there is a generally disconcerted, and at times hysterical, reaction in the West, on the part of some men, to the move towards 'gender equality'. And secondly, representations of women in the media are becoming less sexist, pre-eminently because women are now perceived by businesses as constituting a significant market. As Jones remarks: 'The advertisers are now falling over themselves to portray woman as the all-conquering modern consumer' (20).

To what extent has this 'transformation of gender relations' (and the accompanying male insecurity) manifested itself in

Figure 17   Gudang Garam cigarette advertisement, Indonesia

various cultures in Asia? And how does this tie in with some of the other major issues and contexts (global/local tensions, orientalism, global capitalism, the 'westernising' of Asian cultures) that we have identified as central to identity politics in Asia? One answer to this is to recognise that there is an emerging culture of modernity in Asia to which a far greater number of people than ever before have access, and which is influential in the formation of contemporary identities in Asia, including some which support the traditional image of the 'strong man', as in the Indonesian advertisement for Gudang Garam clove cigarettes (see Figure 17), which depicts the man liking his coffee thick, his music hard and his cigarettes the same as they have always been—strong. It's a call to maintain a traditional masculine image.

But there are images increasingly circulating in Asia, especially in fashion magazines, which present an image of men far less assertive than this. For example, when Ng King Kang launched his book on the gay community and the Internet in Singapore, he produced publicity materials which challenged the cultural spaces normally occupied by these strong 'masculine' images by featuring himself, as shown in Figure 18, on postcards distributed freely all over Singapore.

This blurring of male characteristics, roles and attributes has also impacted upon, and challenged, traditional middle-class discourses of the male but, as demonstrated in an advertisement for India's *Mantra* magazine, shown in Figure 19, 'traditional' male achievements, values and family responsibilities are described as 'cruel fate'. The responsibilities associated with being in relationships (as son, boyfriend, husband, father) are constructed as millstones round the neck of the 'Mantra man', whose sexuality has been overwhelmed by duty. Sexuality and masculinity will be returned to him (for a 'few moments in [his] life'), however, through the process of consumerism—in this case in the form of the 'commodities' available in 'Mantra male-order magazine'. Contrast this with Figure 20, advertising a new Hong Kong magazine simply entitled *Him*. Claiming to offer 'every man's most desirable lifestyle', the images offer fashion, fetishism and even a (stereotyped) nod to gay culture.

GAY AND LESBIAN VOICES

While it is true that media representations such as those discussed above are largely addressed to urban middle- and upper-middle-class contexts, in recent times their influence has spilled over to other areas as well, and increasingly other voices, especially gay and lesbian, are making themselves heard in some

"Life is such a misery, and the term gay, such an irony"...

Figure 18   Free postcard advertising Ng King Kang's
***Rainbow Connection*, Singapore**

parts of Asia, especially through the Internet. A good example is the Website 'Auntie Teck's Home for Lesbians in Asia', covering, in particular, Singapore, Hong Kong, Vietnam, the Philippines, Thailand, Malaysia, Indonesia, Korea, China, Taiwan and Japan. Its goal is 'To encourage visibility and networking of lesbian and bi women in Asia through existing Internet resources . . . to facilitate a connection between isolated lesbians and bi women in Asia and the gay community'.

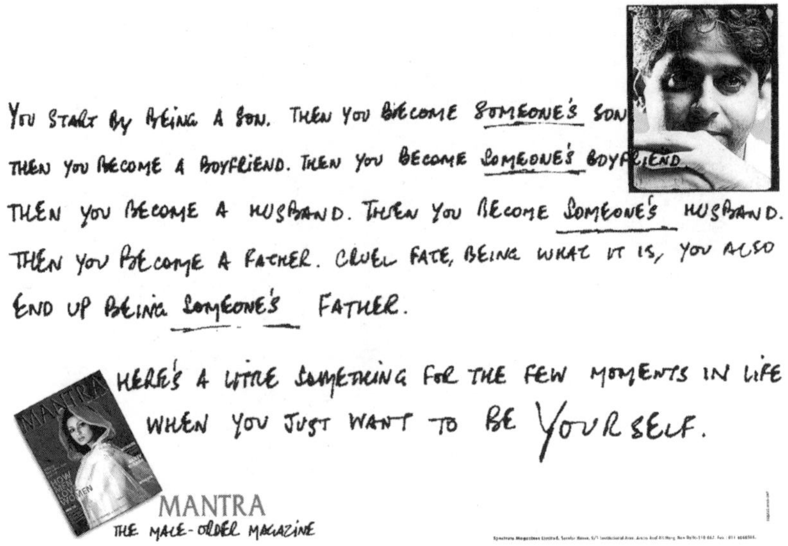

Figure 19 Advertisement for *Mantra*, New Delhi

This is, of course, a mostly middle-class activity—many people in most countries in Asia have little or no contact with the Internet, but where they do, the Internet is rapidly becoming the main public sphere for the building of social capital for alternative, especially gay and lesbian, voices. Ng King Kang, in his extensive study of the Internet in Singapore as a meeting place and forum for the gay community (Ng, 1999), makes that very clear, arguing that virtual space has effectively created a community far stronger and more vocal than has existed before in Singapore. Homosexuality is illegal in Singapore, as indeed it is in most countries in Asia, though their laws (unlike Singapore) may not often expressly state this, leaving gays and lesbians across Asia uncertain about their legal status. As an August 1998 issue of *Asiaweek*, a widely distributed English language magazine in Asia (and beyond), made clear, there is no specific legislation in China, Japan, Indonesia, the Philippines or Thailand. Sodomy and fellatio are illegal in Malaysia, and Singapore forbids 'carnal inter-course against the order of nature with any man, woman or animal'. India, too, bans all 'unnatural acts', including sodomy, although there is now an articulate gay and lesbian discourse

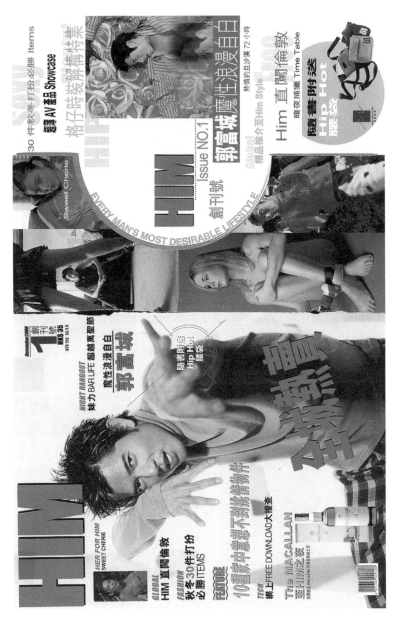

Figure 20 Advertisement for *Him*, Hong Kong

within the country. The legacy of British colonialism has seen the once repressive anti-homosexual laws being maintained for endo-colonialist reasons in India, Malaysia and Singapore in particular (all once British colonies), but Hong Kong (a British colony until 1999) decriminalised homosexual acts in private between consenting adults in 1991, a legacy of the changing laws of the UK (*Asiaweek*, 7 August 1998). Hong Kong is still the only country in Asia to have decriminalised (where laws exist) homosexual acts in private between consenting adults, making possible images like those in Figure 21, the cover and one of the internal images of a comic book available on general release, in which the male heroes are lovers. Such a publication would not be allowed in most other countries of Asia, perhaps with the exception of Japan.

Julian Gearing, in a discussion of transvestites and trans-sexuals in Thailand (*kathoey*), widely assumed in the West to be associated with prostitution, suggests that *kathoey* are tolerated but not accepted. 'For many heterosexuals', he says, 'sex with a *kathoey*, while not openly approved, carries little of the stigma of going with a female prostitute', and it is often quite wrong to assume that the men seeking sex with *kathoey* are gay. But the day-to-day reality is that many of these men and boys do turn to prostitution in order to survive (*Asiaweek*, 7 August 1998). Being *kathoey*, like being gay, is not generally a lifestyle choice, a point many in both the West and in Asia often fail to

Figure 21   Front cover and internal image from *Boy to Boy* comic book, Hong Kong

recognise. As Choong Tet Sieu in *Asiaweek* pointed out, in most places in Asia, perhaps with the exception of the Philippines— which has a thriving and very vocal gay community voice and presence—'the underlying truth about gay life [in Asia] is that there is safety only in numbers', and that 'From Tokyo to Jakarta, homosexuals mostly lead a Jekyll and Hyde existence'. 'Persecution', he suggests, 'has been largely banished, but ostracism has not'. There is not, however, the sort of aggression against gay men, often found in the West, that often results in gay-bashing. As one gay Malay actor in Malaysia explained to Choong Tet Sieu: 'There is no confrontation, no fag-bashing. We can dance together even in straight discos'; although from time to time, in both Malaysia and Singapore, raids are conducted on clubs and bars and there are none that would openly advertise as being gay. Word of mouth (and now Internet posting) is still the way in which gay social capital is built up.

If there is aggressive homophobia in Asia, it comes, according to Hong Kong academic Chou Wah-shan, as a legacy of western imperialism and cultural expansionism although, as *Asiaweek* pointed out, low levels of violence against gays in Asia do not indicate social acceptance of homosexuality or gay communities. The widespread expansion of certain types of Christianity in Asia, with often overtly anti-gay policies and dictates, has been seen to be increasing levels of intolerance, although some gay Christian churches are establishing themselves in certain parts of Asia, as they are in the West. The Hong Kong Blessed Minority Christian Fellowship; the Tong-Kwang Light House Presbyterian Church in Taipei in Taiwan; the Canaan Tongzhi Christian Fellowship in Kaoshiung in Taiwan and the Rainbow Fellowship in Hong Kong are good examples. Although there are no openly gay churches in Singapore, Safehaven is a support group operating for *lesbigay* Christians in Singapore and gay-friendly services are held by the Anglican Garden City Christian Community in the Armenian Church every Saturday. Gay Pride marches have been held in Manila and Bangkok, but these are rare, and when one was held in Taiwan in 1998 many participants wore masks to hide their identities. China, for example, still uses electric shock therapy to 'cure' gay men; and in 1996 Thai Education Minister Sukhavich Rangsitpol described homosexual men as 'sick, both physically and mentally', calling for them to be put into special homes (*Asiaweek,* 7 August 1998).

In an unusual public statement, Senior Minister Lee Kuan Yew, often described as one of the most authoritarian leaders of Asia, when asked about gays in Singapore in a recent CNN interview, replied that his government would not interfere with peoples' lives if they did not openly flaunt themselves, although not long after this the Singaporean promoter of the famous Thai kick-boxer Pirinya was warned by the police because he had not informed them that Pirinya (a famous transvestite in Thailand) would be appearing in drag in a public shopping centre. Drag shows are not banned in Singapore but they are not allowed in places to which children have access and nor are they allowed to 'offend the audience by the exposure of the groin, buttocks or female breasts' (*The Straits Times,* 30 March, 1999). Some Singapore gay men and lesbians are becoming more vocal and organised, but the government refused to licence the group PLU (People Like Us) in 1999, which means that if more than just a few people gather together as PLU it is considered to be an illegal assembly. In Japan there have been some very successful campaigns by gay activists through the group OCCUR, which was set up in 1986 and has a membership running in the tens of thousands but overall, the situation in Asia for gay and lesbian voices to be actively (and openly) contributing to civil society movements is still in its infancy.

However the changes to, and transformations of, gender categories and relations, and their relations with contexts such as globalisation, global capitalism and informationalism, have 'flowed on' to affect the ways in which sexuality, sexual preference and identity are constituted and negotiated in contemporary Asia. Globalisation and informationalism, whatever their negative effects on cultures in Asia, have contributed to these changes, mainly through the 'opening up' of a much more accessible, and less controllable, public sphere.

CONCLUSION

We have considered how gender and sexuality function, both historically and in contemporary contexts, as sites of the imposition, contestation and transformation of certain identities in Asia.

We also suggested that gender issues in Asia are implicated in contemporary processes of modernity, rather than being some simple derivative of an unchanging 'tradition'. In order to position gender—femaleness, maleness, and any other identity that does not neatly fall into this categorisation—within political, historical and social frameworks, we need to see it as a complex and unfolding phenomenon. In our next chapter we will look at the ways in which these same frameworks have contributed to the production and transformation of 'ethnic identities' in contemporary Asia.

SUGGESTIONS FOR FURTHER READING

Chow, Rey (1991) *Woman and Chinese Modernity: The Politics of Reading Between West and East*, University of Minnesota Press, Minneapolis

Grewal, Inderpal and Caren Kaplan (eds) (1994) *Scattered Hegemonies: Postmodernity and Transnational Feminist Practices*, University of Minnesota Press, Minneapolis

Mohanty, Chandra, Ann Russo and Lourdes Torres (1991) *Third World Women and the Politics of Feminism*, Indiana University Press, Bloomington

Trinh T. Minh-ha (1989) *Woman, Native, Other: Writing, Postcoloniality and Feminism*, Indiana University Press, Bloomington

8

Ethnicity

The question of ethnicity and ethnic identities is one of the most important issues in contemporary Asia, mainly because what have been described as 'ethnic tensions' can be found throughout the region, and probably constitute the most serious threat to its political stability and to national sovereignty. In fact the word 'ethnic', as well as supposedly designating a natural community of people (as opposed to artificial nations), has come to be associated with a variety of negative terms and connotations—such as terrorism, anti-modernity, violence, intolerance and ethnic 'cleansing'. In the media these negative connotations are gathered together under the notion of 'tribalism'; which suggests that ethnic groups, and the tensions and violence associated with them, are the products of age-old hatreds and rivalries. In this chapter we look at this 'primordialist' nation of ethnicity, and test it against the evidence of what is happening in contemporary Asia, particularly in the context of the processes of cultural, social and economic globalisation.

PRIMORDIAL ETHNICITY

The idea of ethnicity has usually been defined by political scientists, anthropologists and sociologists in terms of three main characteristics. Firstly, ethnic identities have been understood as relatively small, natural communities that predate nation-states. Secondly, ethnic identity is supposedly based on shared culture and experiences (language, space, history, rituals, dress, food). And thirdly, ethnicity is understood as being based on what we could call 'blood ties'—that is, bio-logical similarities, kinship and skin colour.

This is the version of ethnicity that has been produced and disseminated in the media, particularly after the violence and ethnic cleansing which occurred in the Balkan states. At the same time the disintegration of the former Yugoslavia has had its counterpoints, as far as the media is concerned, in Africa (Sudan), the Pacific (Fiji), the Americas (Mexico) and most particularly in Asia. Malaysia, Indonesia, Pakistan, Thailand, Burma, China, India and Sri Lanka, for instance, have all been subjected to 'ethnic pressures'. As far as the media is concerned, such outbreaks of violence are evidence of a degen-eration of peoples into pre-modern tribal blood-lusting, as evidenced by film of slaughtered victims and fleeing refugees, and interviews with terrified survivors which detail the brutal-ity of the violence (decapitation, torture, mutilation, rape).

When these 'ethnic tensions' are addressed, either by the media or state spokespersons, the characteristics we identified earlier (they are pre-modern, and are based on shared experi-ences and customs, and 'blood ties') are usually transformed into something that is negative and threatening. 'The ethnic' quickly becomes 'the tribal', which is identified with endemic violence and terrorism, irrationality, mass hysteria, and anti-modernity: the 'Thug uprising' in the film *Gunga Din*, to which we referred in Chapter 1, is an example of how some older western cultural texts once understood and represented 'Asian tribalism'. Some still do.

These associations are more or less based on the idea that these groups have rejected the civilising influences of modernity and the Enlightenment project, and everything that goes with it, including tolerance, rationality and reason, a capitalist economy, consumerism, participatory democracy, science, education, civil society, freedom of the press, humanism, liberated sexuality, birth control and a respect for human rights. Such communities are seen as immature and childlike, a mass of largely unthinking people governed by a single ancient mind-set which can only recall and repeat century-old hatreds. This scenario has been played out many times in western popular cultural depictions of

'Asian' societies, with people being represented as robot-like creatures who can burst into irrational violence when manipulated by mad or evil leaders. These stereotypes were very popular during the first half of the twentieth century, when anti-colonialist movements posed a threat to western dominance in Asia, but they have resurfaced, probably as a response to the American debacle in Vietnam, fears about the economic power of the 'Asian tiger' economies, and the potential emergence of China as a player in world affairs.

This attitude is very closely tied to what we described earlier as 'neo-colonialist'. That is, it is based on the presumption that western culture civilises and matures peoples, helping them to grow out of this state of tribalism. The argument that is used to back up this 'primordial' version of ethnicity in Asia and elsewhere is that countries which have accepted, and now practise, western ways are free of 'tribal violence'. The examples that are used include Germany, France, Britain and Scandinavia in Europe, newer 'westernised' nations such as the US, Australia, Canada and New Zealand, and countries in Asia such as Japan, Korea, Hong Kong and Singapore.

This 'neo-colonialist' version of events only makes sense if we accept the idea that ethnicity is a form of irrational blood-lusting. There is a different version of the idea of ethnicity and how it functions in the modern world, put forward by Arjun Appadurai (1997), which both provides evidence against the primordialist approach, and attempts to contextualise ethnicity in terms of the globalising of peoples, politics, culture and capital.

Appadurai rejects the primordialist version of ethnicity simply because it doesn't stand up to the evidence that is available from contemporary Asia, or anywhere else in the world for that matter. The most dubious point, for Appadurai, is that if ethnic groups are blood-lusting, primordial mobs ready to explode, why don't they do it all the time? In other words, if ethnicity is a kind of biologism that can only be cured through immersion in western culture, why are there periods when supposedly 'immature' ethnic communities don't explode into violence?

The connection between supposedly 'mature' communities and westernisation is even more dubious when it is considered that the 'gifts of modernity' supplied by the West (participatory democracy, consumerism, market economy) have, at least in Asia, not produced any obvious decrease in the level of ethnic 'tension'. Further, those 'gifts' have not always translated into the kind of society that reflects Enlightenment principles. After all, countries that have been the recipients of western civilisation have often been characterised by authoritarian politics (South Korea, Indonesia, the Philippines, Taiwan, Singapore), military interventions in political process (South Korea, Indonesia, Taiwan, the Philippines, Pakistan, Thailand) and endemic corruption among politicians and the civil service (the Philippines, India, Pakistan).

The argument that is put to counter these examples is that countries have to undergo a 'hardship period', similar to that currently being experienced by Russia and the other former Soviet satellites, before the full benefits of the Enlightenment can work their effects. Four countries are singled out in Asia—Japan, Singapore, South Korea and Hong Kong—as examples of the necessity for a transition period before westernisation can work its 'magic'. But there are at least two reasons why this position doesn't hold up. Firstly, the four countries cited as 'exemplary' owed their 'success' in no small way, as Manuel Castells points out (and he makes a convincing argument for including the supposedly autonomous Hong Kong in this category), to extensive western economic and military subsidisation or back-up (Castells, 1998). And secondly, none of these countries—not even Japan—has been characteristed by a multi-party, participatory democratic system, allied to a market-driven, non-interventionist economy—a combination that is usually put forward as the basis of the 'western way'.

The argument that western civilising influences lead automatically to a decrease in, or eradication of, 'ethnic discontents' does not even stand up to scrutiny in terms of the supposedly more 'advanced' western countries themselves. The US, Germany, the UK, Australia, New Zealand and France have all had their share, recently, of ethnic tensions. The 'primordial bug' seems to have hit those countries, precisely because they have been relatively economically successful, and have attracted large levels of migration.

What all this points to is the unsustainability of the 'primordial' thesis of ethnicity. In its place, Appadurai has argued for what he calls a culturalist version of ethnicity. He points out that ethnic identities are no more 'natural' than nations. He accepts the primordialist assertion that ethnic groups are characterised by certain things that are shared (language, history, food, rituals, dress), but to this he adds the important point that these 'markers of group identity' have to be mobilised through the creation of a consciousness that values these markers, and the accompanying (ethnic) identity, above all other possible identities (which could be organised, for instance, in terms of nationality, religion, trade unions, political parties, gender, class or occupation). He also adds that these shared features, and the identity that goes with them, mark the ethnic group, first and foremost, as 'different' (to the nation, or to other ethnic groups).

Appadurai adapts Benedict Anderson's ideas about the 'imagining' of nations, and applies them to ethnic groups. He points to the way, for instance, in which the 'creation' of nationalist sentiments actually led to ethnic tensions, but because these were tied in with the 'official' functions of governments and states, they were not recognised as ethnic or tribalist. For instance, the various ethnic tensions in Malaysia are in a sense directly attributable to the state's *Bumiputra* policy which privileges Malays, and which is backed up by the military, government propaganda, laws and the education system; and the same is true of the policy of *Pancasila* in Indonesia, which has been used against ethnic Chinese as well as Islamic groups. The situation in both these countries is not simply explicable in terms of national identity being threatened by ethnic (Chinese, East Timorese) or other discontent. Rather it has at least partially arisen out of the state creation of an 'ethnic monopoly' (an identification of one group with the state) within the nation. The same situation is to be found, to a certain extent, in Japan and India.

Appadurai points to a number of other aspects of contemporary ethnic identities and practices which support the culturalist argument. Ethnic groups, for the most part, are relatively large in number, claim separate nationhood, self-determination, or some kind of autonomy, and are involved in conflict with other large-scale ethnic groups disguised as 'nations'. (Population groups from the north-eastern states of India and Tamils in Sri Lanka fit this description.) Unlike traditional ethnic 'tribes', such groups are not located in one geographical area, but are often spread across different national territories (Sikhs in India and Canada, for instancce), and are increasingly subject to physical dislocations (through diasporic movements, expulsions, migration and refugee flights).

What is being suggested, in effect, is that we are going through a distinctly modern phase of the creation of ethnic identities—and tensions. Two questions are of particular importance: how are ethnic identities and attitudes mobilised in the face of so many difficulties (state opposition, physical dislocation), and what part does social, political, cultural and economic globalisation play in this process?

ETHNICITIES AS IMAGINED COMMUNITIES

We made the point earlier that the creation of ethnicity comes about through the conversion of a set of shared features (a culture) into a consciousness of identity which, for a very large group of people (sometimes scattered across the world), is the 'only' identity that matters (that is, is important enough to cause people to give up their lives, or to take the lives of others). Ethnicities, like nations, are 'imagined' into existence through two main conditions—mass literacy, and the spread of the mass media. Again we have to go back and see how, according to Benedict Anderson, nation states used these two factors to weld together disparate groups of people through the repetition, in all aspects of everyday life, of ideological narratives of community, belonging and identity. The fact of mass literacy meant that more and more people could be targeted—through newspapers, cartoons, pamphlets, posters, books—with messages that reinforced ideas of common bloodlines, history, traditions, language, values, religion and destiny. The same scenario applies, today, to notions of ethnicity (we noted before that nationalism was merely ethnicity officially writ large), except that the spread of the mass media to incorporate newer visual media (computers, videos, satellite television) means that delivery of these ideas is faster, more powerful (because of the 'credibility' of visual images), and able to overcome physical dislocation.

Of late, anthropologists have provided excellent accounts of the manner of the construction of ethnic identities in Asia in the context of modernity, globalisation, and the rise of a new middle class in many societies in Asia. Joel Kahn has noted that the past few decades in Malaysia have witnessed the involvement of a 'growing middle class' in the constitution of a 'Malay culture industry' (Kahn, 1992: 164). An idea of 'traditional (that is, rural) Malay culture' as the 'real' Malaysia has sought to be instituted through contexts as diverse as 'domestic tourist and leisure markets, the contemporary arts and architecture, the government-sponsored handicraft industry, popular magazines and newspapers, advertising copy, museum layout' etc. (Kahn, 1992: 163). Kahn notes that in many such instances Malaysian culture comes to refer primarily to just one ethnic group, the Malays, and that 'many of these images . . . represent Malay culture in a feudal and patriarchal manner' (164). The complexities of the situation—modernity, globalisation, and consumerism—in which ideas of 'real' Malay culture are sought to be instituted are well captured in the following paragraph:

> Ironically, the revived interest in a traditional, rurally-based Malay Culture is taking place in a social setting characterised by a massive decline in what is considered to be the traditional Malay peasant community. This produces some fascinating paradoxes. The images generated by this culture industry in travel brochures, museums, newspapers, magazines, books and films depict Malay villagers as philosophical players of Malay games and fliers of kites, who like nothing better than dance dramas depicting the life of the Malay court. In my time in a Malay village in the mid 1970s I never once say anyone flying a kite or playing [the local game of] congkak. And the villagers I knew had little interest in the performances of 'traditional' Malay dance drama currently being staged in luxury hotels in Kuala Lumpur, preferring instead to watch *Dallas* and *The Professionals* on television. Traditional Malay wedding gear, a favoured display at local cultural centres, was rejected by village brides who favoured platform shoes and blue taffeta (Kahn 1992: 164).

As this example indicates, ethnicity, like national identity, has to be both 'imagined' into existence, and continually reinforced. And just as with nationalism, mass literacy and the mass media are the means through which narratives of 'ethnic belonging' are made available to large numbers of people. But what is the process that, firstly, turns a shared culture into an identity, and secondly, provokes the outbreak of mass violence that the media has labelled 'tribalism'? One good explanation for this is associated with the French sociologist Pierre Bourdieu (Bourdieu, 1991).

We referred earlier to Bourdieu's notion of habitus, which can be defined, very generally, as a set of learned dispositions which change with a person's social and cultural trajectory (for instance, from family to school to university to work). Each context places a different emphasis on what is considered valuable or natural, and a person gradually incorporates these values, and the 'bodily hexis' that goes with them (dress, ways of moving, spatial protocols, ways of 'seeing' the body). This is one of the ways nations (and ethnic groups), through the dissemination of images and ideas, both code a person's identity (a Singaporean citizen will dress neatly, and will not spit in public), and make sure that identity can be checked and regulated (cameras record people's behaviour in lifts, or in public spaces). In this age of transnationalism and globalisation people are confronted with many different 'embodied identities' (in 'foreign' films, television shows, books, cartoons, video games, computer material). What this means is that these embodied identities have to be more aggressively marketed, disseminated and monitored in order to 'withstand the competition' from global consumer culture. But as can be seen from Figures 22 and 23, the effect of western culture and advertising on different ethnic groups is still highly pervasive. In Figure 22, the western ideal of female beauty is being promoted, with Asian women being encouraged to buy an American product that will increase the size of their breasts, while Figure 23 demonstrates the longevity of the UK punk scene, with a current Hong Kong teen band decked out in an approximation of a style which probably reached its peak before they were born.

This awareness of embodied identities leads to our second point, about the eruptions of ethnic violence. Firstly, as we have seen, there is already a great deal of 'ethnic violence' perpetrated in the name of legitimate state action (in East Timor or Tibet, for instance, where Indonesia and China denied 'ethnic' groups the right to self-determination; or in the

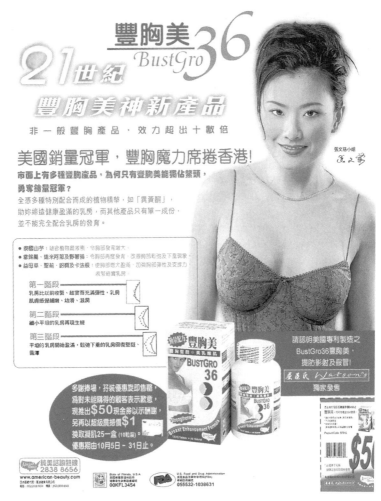

Figure 22   'BustGro' advertisement, *Oriental Sunday*, 2000

military action against separatist groups in Thailand, Cambodia and Myanmar), which, when it is reciprocated, is labelled 'tribalism'.

Secondly, given the enormous pressures ethnic identities are under (from the state, and from global culture), the processes of creating an ethnic consciousness have to set up that culture 'against' something else—which threatens its existence, denies its aspirations and denies its humanity. This is what some

Figure 23   Teen band, *Yes! Idol* magazine, Hong Kong

psychoanalysts call 'identity as difference'—my existence comes into being when someone else 'stands in the way' of my self-determination, my values, my destiny, my pleasure, my way of life. Think of the way in which Croatian identity, for instance, is (at least currently) totally dependent on 'not being Serbian or Yugoslavian'. And much the same could be said of the ethnic tensions in East Timor and Tibet.

What we have then, in the contemporary world, is a situation where peoples are increasingly made to feel rootless, alienated and psychologically distanced. The creation of ethnic identities—in opposition to some 'other' group—is done through valuing 'our culture' as natural and human, and 'the other' culture as degenerate, threatening and, increasingly, non-human (which accounts, to some extent, for the scale and level of the violence in ethnic disputes). And this process has been exacerbated as nation-states (themselves disguised ethnicities) and national sovereignties are put under increased pressure by the various aspects of globalisation.

ETHNICITY, STATE SOVEREIGNTY AND GLOBALISATION

We made the point earlier that this tendency towards 'ethnic tensions' is in many ways a relatively modern development, tied up with the proliferation of the traditional mass media (newspapers, radio, film, television) and more recent mass communication technology (computers, satellite television and the Internet). Why? The sovereignty of national states, in Asia and elsewhere, is being threatened and eroded because they are unable to control and regulate a number of crucial areas, particularly finance/economics (monetary exchange rates, levels of unemployment, tariffs, interest rates), but also other areas such as information flows, social relations, laws (civic and corporate), national borders, foreign policies, labour relations and ownership of raw materials, businesses and utilities, including the media. Adding to these pressures is the condition of what Appadurai calls 'ethnoscapes' (Appadurai, 1997), which can be described as a kind of globalising of ethnicity. National borders are increasingly being breached by waves of population shifts (migrants, refugees, guest workers), while supposedly homogeneous local cultures and identities, carefully created and 'naturalised' through the 'imagining of nationhood', are subject to ethnic challenges (in the areas of language, ritual, values, religion).

The flow of peoples, information and capital that characterises globalisation tends toward the undermining of national sovereignty, which invariably produces a redoubling of the effort to maintain national control and regulation (for example, Internet surveillance and control in China and Singapore). In other words, the issue of 'national identity' is accentuated to an even greater extent (for instance, in Indonesia, China, Malaysia), while the 'enemies of the nation' are singled out, officially or otherwise, for retribution. The anti-Chinese riots in Indonesia constitute an obvious example of this process. The threats to national sovereignty posed by the Asian economic crisis, the fall in value of the rupiah, and the intervention of world economic bodies (the World Bank and the International Monetary Fund), resulted in 1998–99, in murderous riots directed against the Chinese population as a whole, and particular Chinese businesspeople, who conveniently 'stood in' for those global forces which Indonesia and Indonesians have no way of controlling. In other words, Indonesians deprived of jobs or faced with starvation 'took their plight' out on a group—the Chinese—who could be conveniently identified and designated as either part of the problem, and/or as somehow immune from the suffering.

The more the state increases its efforts to identify scapegoats (during his leadership President Soeharto of Indonesia, for instance, more or less countenanced, at different times, outbreaks of violence against ethnic Chinese), and to homogenise national culture and identity, the greater the likelihood of opposition, disruptions and 'ethnic violence'. Michel Foucault points out that the exercising of power (by way of the normalisation, control and regulation of peoples and practices) always produces a variety of 'others'—in this case, those who do not fit into the homogenised 'identity-kit' produced by state ideologies and discourses (Foucault, 1997). However, in what looks very much like a case of 'entropy' in the political and social sphere, the more the state exercises its control, the more control escapes it, as Appadurai writes:

> . . . the failure of nation-states to control and define the lives of their citizens is writ large in the growth of shadow economies, private and quasi-private armies and constabularies, secessionary nationalism, and a variety of non-governmental organisations that provide alternatives to the national control of the means of subsistence and justice (1997: 189–90).

This failure manifests itself in secessionary movements in India, Indonesia, Myanmar, Nepal, Pakistan and the Philippines, among others, and in the mushrooming of privately organised militia based on caste lines (such as the upper caste *Ranvir sena* in the east Indian state of Bihar). However, in some cases these developments, while challenging the authority of the state, manifest similar pretensions to authoritarianism as the state itself.

ETHNICITIES AND GLOBAL CAPITAL

While there is obviously a strong connection, promoted by the media, between ethnicity and violence (terrorism, pogroms, organised crime), there is another aspect to contemporary ethnicity that generally escapes media attention, and that is the relationship between ethnic networks and global capital. In the third volume of his series on the information age, *End of*

Millennium, Manuel Castells writes about a study he conducted on ethnic Chinese business networks and capital investment in China (Castells, 1998). His findings provide a completely different perspective on ethnicity in Asia (different to the media-popularised one of destabilisation, terrorism and violence), and they demonstrate that there is an 'ethnically localised' dimension to the practices of global capitalism.

Castells conducted his study on the extent to which investment in China, particularly in the southern economic zones, was tied to 'ethnic networking'. He found that a high percentage of foreign investment in areas such as the Zhejiang Delta came from businesspeople in Taiwan and Hong Kong, who were faced with rising production costs at home, and were attracted by the low production costs and potentially high profitability (although also high risk) associated with Chinese ventures.

His study identified not only that a high level of investment in China came from overseas Chinese, but also that this investment largely worked through what he called *guanxi* (relationship) networks, based on associations of kinship, geographical origins, or dialect groups. Hong Kong firms, for instance, utilised these ethnic networks in investing in and/or building hotels, business services, airports, roads and property development, and were particularly active in the new enterprise zone of Pudong (centred in Shanghai). Capital flowed into this, and other economic zones, from ethnic Chinese business-people in Singapore, Bangkok, Penang, Kuala Lumpur, Jakarta, California, New York, Canada and Australia.

In one sense this flow of investment into China epitomised the notion of globalised capital, but with a specifically localised inflection, being based on ethnic networks (which are often familial) which usually work through Hong Kong firms. 'The statistical pre-eminence of Hong Kong is', according to Castells, 'a mirage', simply reflecting:

> ... the management of plural sources of investment by Hong Kong-based Chinese firms. It should be interpreted as 'global capital'. But this 'global capital', which can be, and is, from any source, from Japanese banks to money launderers, is administered, and to a large extent controlled, by Chinese business networks, more often than not based on

family relationships, and inter-linked among themselves, in spite of fierce rivalry in specific markets and projects (Castells, 1998: 297).

This relationship, Castells argues, does not simply involve business firms. 'Ethnic connections' extend through local and provincial governments in China, involving the 'bureaucratic entrepreneurs' who facilitate and promote Chinese economic development (297). What Castells' study evidences is that, at least as far as the Chinese experience is concerned, the whole process of globally driven economic development works through, and is substantially dependent upon, ethnic networks.

CONCLUSION

The 'ethnic question', in Asia and elsewhere, has usually been dealt with in terms of explanations based on notions of primordialism and tribalism. Such explanations do not stand up to contemporary evidence. Rather 'ethnicity' needs to be understood very much along the lines of Anderson's theory of nations as 'imagined communities', communities which are often produced out of tensions associated with various nation-alist projects. What we are dealing with in contemporary Asia is a largely modern version of 'ethnic consciousness' which cannot be understood without regard to the relationship between national sovereignty and globalisation, on the one hand and, on the other, the interaction between local and global networks. One of the other major consequences of glo-balisation, and an equally significant player in the interaction between local and global networks in Asia, is the increase in the number and breadth of diasporic movements. In our final chapter we look at how global forces are giving rise to 'little Asias' throughout the world—a kind of Asia without borders.

SUGGESTIONS FOR FURTHER READING

Bhabha Homi K. (ed.) (1990) *Nation and Narration*, Routledge, London and New York
—(1994) *The Location of Culture*, Routledge, London and New York

ASIA

Gandhi, Leela (1998) *Postcolonial Theory*, Allen & Unwin, Sydney; Columbia University Press, New York; Edinburgh University Press, Edinburgh

Kahn, Joel (1995) *Culture, Multiculture, Postculture*, Sage, London

Perera, Suvendrini (ed.) (1995) *Asia and Pacific Inscriptions: Identities, Ethnicities, Nationalities*, Meridian, Melbourne

9

Asia without borders

The contemporary increase in diasporic movements (that is, the relocation and dispersal of large groups of people sharing a common identity based on such things as race, ethnicity or nationality) is part of a much wider process of 'deterritorialisation' associated with globalisation, and of worldwide capital and information flows, as well as the tensions and problems arising out of ethnic and religious separatist movements. All these developments have one major effect in common: they place considerable strain on the sovereignty of the state. In other words, they make it difficult for nation-states to perform their traditional functions (associated with the control, regulation and care of populations) with the same effectiveness and authority.

Asia is no stranger to diasporas, both in terms of groups located within, and living outside, different national borders in Asia. For the past thousand years or so travellers from different parts of Asia have been wandering in and out of different regions, bringing back stories of different customs, different religious practices, different worlds, etc. An interesting example of an ancient diasporic movement concerns the Jewish settlements on the northwestern frontier of India dating from pre-Islamic times (from the eighth century onwards). By the tenth century, there is firm historical evidence to indicate the presence of large numbers of Jews in many cities such as Nishapur, Maimanah, Herat and Kandahar. The northwest region in which these cities and towns lay was referred to as

Khorasan, and the so-called 'Khorasanian Jewish settlements' maintained trade connections with Europe, India, China, the Islamic Middle East and North Africa. This trade diaspora was, at the time, the largest existing in the world, constituting a single network and a shared cosmopolitan culture (Wink, 1987: 360).

There are sizeable Indian populations in Singapore, Malaysia and Hong Kong, Chinese in Malaysia, Papua New Guinea and Indonesia, Vietnamese in Australia, France and the US, and Filipinos in the Arab states and Hong Kong. At the same time there are Asian diasporas scattered throughout the world, with the Chinese in various cities in the US, and in countries such as Britain and Australia; Indians in the US, Canada, Fiji, Britain, Africa, the West Indies and throughout the Gulf states; and Koreans in Japan and Los Angeles.

DETERRITORIALISATION

Arjun Appadurai puts forward the argument—and it is one supported by other theorists in this field, such as Ulf Hannerz (1996)—that diasporas 'are part of the cultural dynamic of urban life in most countries and continents, in which migration and mass mediation constitute a new sense of the global as modern and the modern as global (1997: 10). There are a number of reasons for this development. We have already mentioned that national sovereignty is under pressure from transnational and multinational corporations, and world financial organisations, which have become significant players in decision-making processes (in Papua New Guinea with the Bougainville Panguna copper mine, in Indonesia and Korea with the International Monetary Fund's intervention in economic policy formulation). Decisions about the interrelationship between social and economic issues are no longer necessarily the domain of national or state governments. Global markets and capital flows are having a destabilising effect on the social fabric of places, and their accompanying demographics.

For example, Unocal, a large company headquartered in California with an annual turnover of more than US$6 billion from operations in over twenty countries, has been heavily criticised by many in the west for returning to operate in

Myanmar following the lifting of a government ban on foreign firms operating there in 1987. Myanmar is currently ruled by a military junta that refuses to recognise legitimate election victories and which has held opposition leader Aung San Suu Kyi under house arrest since 1990. Unocal operated in Myanmar (or Burma, as it was then) for many years until the Ne Win nationalist government forced all foreign firms to leave. Unocal has faced worldwide boycotts because of its decision to return to what is seen to be a very repressive state, but in partnership with French oil company Total was committed to building a 254-mile natural gas pipeline through the country to Thailand. Much of this passes through Karen territory and has caused major difficulties for that minority ethnic group, many of whom have been displaced, their villages razed to the ground, and their way of life overturned.

Throughout all of this Unocal has argued that it is politically neutral and that it has been helping the infrastructure of Myanmar by building schools and clinics, and having an overall 'net positive impact on the people of that country' (Schwartz & Gibb, 1999: 36). Despite denying that it is complicit with the military government, both Unocal's remaining in Myanmar and also all of the criticisms of it doing so raise important issues about whose values should be followed in making decisions (and judgements) about such things. Arguing for political neutrality is rather simplistic—if globalisation and the impact of large multinational/transnational companies like Unocal on local communities demonstrates anything, it demonstrates the need for us to recognise that nothing we ever do is neutral or disinterested, everything we do is always motivated and contingent, as Pierre Bourdieu would put it. The issue is what we decide to be important, and that will generally mean very different things for very different people.

When the chief executive officer of Nike can earn well in excess of US$1.5 million a year, and a worker in a factory in China making Nike products would have to work nine hours a day, six days a week for 1500 years to earn the same amount (Schwartz & Gibb, 1999: 83), the issue of contingency and different meanings for different people is sharply focused. The average labour costs for producing a pair of Nike trainers in China, the Philippines and Thailand is less than US$1.50, but they sell, often, for hundreds of dollars. The impact of globalisation in these areas is very one-sided. But it does not have to be like this. The Bata shoe company, for example, works closely with the Thai Business Initiative in Rural Development and has set up numerous small shoe factories in poor villages in northern Thailand. These factories are cooperatively owned and managed and profits are put back into the local community (Schwartz & Gibb, 1999: 85). Given that there is only one Asian company listed in the world's top twenty brands (Sony, from Japan), the impact of global western business on local communities is immense, and the flow of capital into different areas, or the decision of corporations to target or bypass locations, can create localised economic booms or depressions almost overnight.

Populations are responding to these developments by becoming extremely mobile, and are moving to areas (both inside and outside national borders) where work can be found. There are also the pressures and tensions associated with ethnic and religious separatism, which can make life extremely difficult and dangerous for large diasporic communities (think of the experience of the Chinese community in Indonesia, and the race riots that accompanied the financial crisis in 1997–98).

IDENTITIES IN ASIA AND DIASPORIC COMMUNITIES

Malaysia, Papua New Guinea and Indonesia all are home to diasporic Chinese communities, who tend to play a very significant role in the local economies. In Malaysia, the issue of the Chinese diaspora is kept out of sight as much as possible, although there are a number of laws and regulations which specifically discriminate against that community in favour of ethnic Malays. In Papua New Guinea the Chinese community runs most of the local businesses, and wields considerable economic power. Like the Chinese in Malaysia, they are seen, largely unofficially, as a potential destabilising force in the country.

Theorists talk about these developments as forms of deterritorialisation. What this means is that the attachment between communities and places is becoming less secure and certain. We know local places are being 're-made' by global forces, which are forcing people to shift places. At the same time, however, those 'shifted' people are then subject to 'foreign' influences (in terms of ideas, values, goods, politics, religious ideas, family structures, languages) which feeds back into their original places and communities. In other words, political systems, economies, cultures and societies in Asia and elsewhere are subject to challenges and influences from obvious sources such as capital and information flows, worldwide media links and world organisations, but they are also being affected through their relations with diasporic communities both at home and overseas. If the biggest issues for contemporary Asian nations is their ability to meet and cope with the challenges of modernity and postmodernity, without losing or compromising their own sense of identity or national sovereignty, then the question of the relation between identities and diasporic communities warrants attention.

This situation is even more dramatically evident in Indonesia—as the 1965 massacre of Chinese (in the Soeharto 'counter-revolution') attests. In February 1998 television screens around the world showed pictures of Indonesian mobs rampaging through towns burning Chinese businesses and houses, and murdering their occupants. The then President Soeharto appeared to give some kind of tacit support to these activities, suggesting that the Indonesian people were simply reacting against those (unnamed) groups who were exploiting them, and for a time the Indonesian army seemed reluctant to step in and protect the Chinese community.

What these examples clearly demonstrate is that the politics of diasporic communities is strongly informed by economic considerations, either real or imagined. Things are far more complex, however, than being reducible to a question of diasporic communities exercising undue economic influence in their host country.

There are a number of possible economic ramifications tied up with diasporic movements. In Australia and New Zealand, for instance, certain residential areas in major cities (Sydney, Auckland) suddenly increased in value because of an influx of 'nervous capital' from Hong Kong prior to the handover to China. Those families that decided to move to, and buy properties in, those cities rather than stay in Hong Kong inadvertently boosted real estate prices and values in the areas they settled in. Generally, however, this has not been the trend worldwide, or in Asia. Areas inhabited by diasporic communities tend to lose value.

There is also a gender dimension to this increase in diasporic movements. In recent years, scholars have begun to speak of the 'feminisation of poverty' as an important aspect of the condition of women in many parts of the world. This is also true of Asia, and refers to the situation where, within a general context of social, cultural and material deprivation, women are the most disadvantaged. The term highlights the linkage between poverty and gender. Let us consider some specific examples.

Many Asian women from poor backgrounds are employed as domestic help in many wealthy Asian households, as well as in several Gulf region countries. So, for example, it is estimated that there are approximately 60 000 Filipinas working as domestic labour in Singapore alone (Matsui, 1999: 47). In effect these women are commoditised and treated as property—as advertisements for maids, 'sold' in newspaper columns like cars or other commodities, make clear (see Figure 24).

A common theme among the many stories of exploitation at the hands of employers is that of physical and sexual abuse. Ironically, the most common way in which such stories come to light is through the media attention on women driven to acts of violence upon their employers whose depredations leave no other avenue of recourse. These include sexual violence, the breaking of conditions of contract, and lack of privacy and personal freedom.

We should, in this context, consider the relationship between the state and women and ask whether women have become just another export commodity for some nation-states in Asia, their extraterritorial welfare being accorded the same low priority that it has received within the sphere of national affairs. And, to the concept of 'feminisation of poverty' in Asia, we may well add the equally dubious category of the 'feminisation of migration', for approximately '72 per cent of women migrant workers in the world are Asian' (1995 Report of Radhika Coomaraswamy, Un Special Rapporteur on Violence against Women, in Matsui, 1999).

We made the point earlier that gender relations, both in Asia and elsewhere, are often predicated on a notion of male identity being bound up with the possession, exchange and control of women: this control of women's sexuality by men is

Figure 24   A selection of advertisements for maids in
The Straits Times, Singapore

seen to be a fundamental aspect of patriarchy. In some parts of Asia, this seems to have found a particularly invidious expression through the prevalence of the so-called 'traffic in women' (Matsui, 1999). Briefly, this refers to the forced employment of migrant women from poorer countries (such as Thailand, Indonesia, Nepal, Sri Lanka and the Philippines) as sex workers in wealthy ones (such as Japan and Taiwan), as well as in the relatively better off ones (such as India). An important context for this traffic is the globalisation of the world economy that has severely impoverished some nations, many of whose citizens are often reduced to situations of absolute powerlessness. It has been estimated that in Japan the 'industry' generates over 4 trillion yen (US$30 billion) annually (Matsui, 1999: 19), and that 5000–7000 Nepalese women are sold into prostitution every year in India.

Extreme poverty is an important context for this situation: and it produces population 'flows' both across and within national borders. Many young women and girls are lured away from their villages with promises of employment in factories in urban areas, only to find that they have 'incurred a debt' to a brothel owner who has 'purchased' them from an 'agent'. This debt, in turn, 'must' be repaid through their work as prostitutes. There is another important aspect to this: the activities of international bodies such as the World Bank often impact severely upon the most vulnerable sections in some societies in Asia, and this, in turn, translates into the severest form of disadvantage for women in these societies.

The keenness of the young women to believe stories of gainful employment in a distant city should, then, also be placed in the context of global economic and political processes through which women are placed in impossible situations of deprivation. The tragedy of this situation is further heightened when one considers that the most common source of transmission of HIV-AIDS in Asia is through heterosexual activity, and that women sex workers in Asia are usually powerless to insist that their clients practise safe sex. Hence, for example, 'the majority of HIV-positive people in northern Thailand are women working in prostitution' (Matsui, 1999: 35).

We need, then, to develop a critical perspective on the processes of globalisation, one that appears to be lacking in, say, popular media analyses which tend to concentrate on technological and financial innovations. In terms of its late twentieth-century manifestation, globalisation has also inflicted unimaginable miseries upon many in its guise as the progressive engine of late capitalism; 'from the destruction of rainforests and the intercontinental dumping of toxic wastes to global warming; [and] the growing transnational trade in human organs for transplant' (Hannerz, 1996: 17). During this time of growing global interaction, Hannerz notes, we have also witnessed 'the tragedy of the Fourth World of aboriginal peoples [in that] it was mostly forced into retreating before that expansion of the First, Second and Third Worlds which again and again destroyed its environment' (18).

CULTURE AND IDENTITY

Diasporic communities generally tend to move to areas where work is relatively freely available. Even allowing for the fact that they often take on the less well-paid jobs (as cleaners, working in restaurants, cafes or food stalls, as maids or manual workers, or in sweat shops), they are usually still able to generate enough income to send money to their families back home. This 'income from abroad' is often vital to local communities, not just in terms of providing food and shelter, but in enabling families to start businesses, or children to receive formal education. This also tends to increase the circulation of 'exotic' goods, both in their adopted homeland, and in the area they have left (by sending goods home, or by taking goods back when they visit).

How do diasporas contribute to global cultural flows and transformations? In many ways, what is happening in the sphere of culture mirrors the kinds of exchanges that occur in the economic sphere. The diasporic communities are themselves caught up in, and influenced by, the cultural products that surround them—and they extend this influence when they send videos, computer games, magazines and newspapers back to their home communities. At the same time they bring into their adopted home a variety of cultural genres and products (Indian and Chinese films, for instance) which feed into, and influence local cultural forms and genres.

At this stage we have only dealt with the cultural aspect of diasporas in terms of the exchange of cultural commodities—

films, clothes, games, food and the like. But there is a far more important dimension to this question, and that is tied up with the notion of identity—of the diasporic community, its hosts, and the community from where it originated.

It is inevitable that once a group moves into a foreign location, a number of factors will influence its cultural identity. Probably the two most important of these are their relationship with the original homeland and people, and the extent to which the diasporic community's cultures—understood here as their way of life, forms of communication, expectations, familial relations, ideas and meanings—are able to be maintained in the face of intense pressure from their new cultural contexts.

The English cultural critic Stuart Hall (in Williams and Chrisman, 1994) suggests that there have been two scenarios put forward to describe this process. In the first of these, what we will call the 'scenario of coherence', diasporic communities share a notion of themselves which is closely tied to, and ultimately determined by, the idea of the 'motherland' or home community. These diasporic communities are characterised by common codes of meaning, values, languages and expectations which are maintained through the inspiration provided by an idealised home culture. The motherland—or at least their idealised version of it—determines how families work, what clothes are worn or food consumed, how people think of themselves and to whom they owe their loyalties and allegiances. In this scenario, there is a homogeneous and stable version of group identity which can always be measured against, and guaranteed by, the mirror of the homeland (the Quebeçois in Canada could be seen in this light). Attempts to integrate or assimilate into local communities, or to take on their cultures, are strongly resisted. Personal identity is almost completely determined by the idea of a pure, original group identity which is tied up with the locality of the homeland and its conventions, values and rituals.

In her analysis of contemporary Indian films the sociologist Patricia Uberoi notes that these have become 'an important site for engagement with the problems resulting from middle-class diaspora, and for the articulation of Indian identity in a globalised world' (Uberoi, 1998: 305). So, recent Indian films have addressed the issue of the parental wish to 'pass on' the 'traditions' and 'values' of Indian culture to their children at the same time that the latter 'continue to enjoy the material and professional benefits of expatriate living' (Uberoi, 1998: 308). In the majority of cases, the films conclude by presenting a conservative agenda for the maintenance of 'Indian traditions' in a globalised context; that is, the 'family is construed as a patriarchal institution' (Uberoi, 1998: 332), through a validation of the rights of males over females, of husbands over wives and of parents (usually fathers) over children.

The second version of diasporas can be described as the 'scenario of negotiated difference'. Here the motherland still exercises a strong influence over how the people see themselves, but this identification is tempered by assimilating local ways of doing things, and expectations are rethought in terms of the opportunities—particularly in the areas of education and career—offered by the new locality. The British comedy series *Goodness Gracious Me!*, made by second- and third-generation south Asians, is perhaps an example of the negotiation of new identities in a global world. It simultaneously critiqued the idea of 'traditional' Indian culture and asserted the right to be different from the majority British culture.

THE DIASPORIC HABITUS

The most important aspect of this scenario is that identity becomes much more self-conscious. In order to follow through on this point, Hall (in Williams and Chrisman, 1994) makes use of Bourdieu's notion of habitus. We introduced the notion of habitus earlier in order to explain how the processes of globalisation were impacting on the lives and practices of people. Hall does something similar with regard to diasporas. He argues that in normal circumstances changes to habitus are very slow and almost undetectable. However in diasporic communities, people are confronted with three contexts which radically change things. Firstly, it is difficult to maintain an unconscious adherence to values and ideas when you are always being confronted with another set of values—that is, a completely different habitus—as part of your everyday life. Bourdieu argues that the habitus is effective because it is largely unchallenged (Bourdieu, 1991). This is not the case with diasporic communities. Secondly, not only do diasporic communities come into contact with an alternative habitus, but in most cases that alternative is far more frequently adhered to. In other words, it is the norm. And thirdly and concomitantly, diasporic communities are aware of the politics of having the 'wrong' habitus—at best it means becoming second-class citizens, at worst it might mean official or unofficial persecution.

According to Hall, these three contexts change the way the habitus operates in diasporas. Instead of being inflexible and continuous, the diasporic habitus is self-conscious, open to political manipulation or persuasion, and always in the process of being improvised. This does not mean that the original habitus, and the identification with the motherland, are cast aside. It just means that this adherence is far more pragmatic. Whereas in our first scenario the motherland dictated behaviour and identity, in the second version its appeal and power are more symbolic or nostalgic.

Hall argues that although the first scenario constitutes the official version of diasporic identity, the second, more pragmatic version is usually the reality. Why? Because members of diasporic communities are continually renegotiating their habitus. They are exposed to new ideas, knowledge, desires and educational opportunities, and pressured to fit in to their new home because markers of 'foreignness' (such as dress and language) can make them targets of bigotry.

The other factor that Hall cites as extremely important is the media. If the motherland still plays the role of a mirror for diasporas, the media is gradually usurping this function. In other words, while the control or influence of the motherland can be exerted through the use of cultural texts (tapes of Islamic holy men calling the faithful to prayer, videos of films, and books outlining familial etiquettes, all take the place of 'the real thing'), communities—particularly its younger members—are likely to be exposed to and influenced by the narratives, fashions, expectations and lifestyles that are found on television, or in magazines. The imaginary community that is held together, to a greater or lesser extent, by a nostalgic longing for an original homeland and lifestyle, is always competing with the imagined community found in the media— which is much closer, more insistent, more glamorous, and more of an inescapable, everyday presence.

What are the ramifications for diasporic communities caught between these two imagined communities? Appadurai (1997) picks out one aspect of community life and identity as being particularly vulnerable—familial relations. In non-diasporic communities, the destabilising influences exerted on families and familial structures by the media and global capitalism is to some extent countered by the continuities of time and place. In other words, the habitus of a community is largely reaffirmed by the cyclical relations between everyday life and cultural institutions—people go to the marketplace and pray at the temple; or in terms of gender, women work in the home or the fields, while men have businesses to go to, or meet in cafes.

In diasporic communities, however, relations between time and place are changed, and the habitus is continually called into question. Appadurai makes the point that although diasporic communities usually move in search of work, often it is the women who end up with the best paying jobs, or sometimes the only jobs. This both erodes the capacity of men to 'control' their families, and calls into question their status and honour. Further, one aspect of educational opportunities being made available to the children of diasporic communities is that they are likely to be far more literate (technically, and in a more general, cultural sense) and, as a result, to have greater access to financial and cultural capital, than is the case with their parents. Both these factors—the challenge to the validity of structured gender relations, and the accumulation of various literacies by children who are theoretically subject to the relatively non-literate parents—contribute to the motherland functioning more as a nostalgic and symbolic, rather than a controlling, influence on diasporic identities.

CONCLUSION

Diasporas constitute both a relatively inescapable everyday reality in contemporary, globalised Asia, and a potential source of instability. Diasporic communities benefit from their new location, and contribute socially, culturally and economically to their host countries. At the same time they bring change, difference, discontinuity and rupture to themselves, their hosts, and to their homeland. Hall points out that the diasporic phenomenon constitutes a distinctive challenge to the habitus—in both its diasporic and local manifestations. During times of relative prosperity and stability this challenge can be accommodated without too much difficulty. However during times of stress or threat, diasporic communities are invariably singled out as the causes of instability.

Diasporic communities both influence, and are transformed by, their host communities. At the same time they are playing an increasingly important role in shaping the directions of cultural politics 'back home'. Their intercourse with home communities can't help but contribute to the transformation of local cultures. At the same time, however, their own nostalgia for a 'traditional past' can act as a strongly conservative force, and even work to exacerbate cultural, social and political tensions that are already likely to be under considerable strain (the link between diasporic communities and increases in Hindu fundamentalism is one example of this phenomenon).

The relation between diasporas and their home communities constitutes one of many aspects of what Partha Chatterjee refers to as 'this unresolved struggle between the narratives of capital and community within the discursive space of the modern state' (Chatterjee, 1993: 239). This book has attempted to trace this relation, specifically apropos of con-temporary Asia, with reference to contexts as 'modern' as globalisation and informationalism, and sites as (supposedly) 'traditional' as religion, gender and ethnicity. To bring to light some of the complexities and contingencies of this relation, and the ways in which groups have negotiated its consequences and imperatives, is to call into question western stereotypes and myths of Asia and 'Asian' identity, and, in the words of Chen Kuan-Hsing, to take on (in a small way) the 'political and intel-lectual responsibility to move forward in fulfilling the incomplete project of decolonization' (Chen, 1998: 47).

This also requires that while we recognise the importance of globalisation as a factor in contemporary life, we should be wary of terms such as 'global village', for it suggests 'not only interconnectedness but, probably to many of us, a sense of greater togetherness, of immediacy, and reciprocity in relation-ships, a very large scale idyll' (Hannerz, 1996: 6). 'The world', Hannerz further points out, 'is not much like that' (6); the process of decolonisation has not left behind a homogeneous space which can now simply be understood through concepts such as 'global village'.

Finally, it is apparent that globalisation is perceived by many as posing a threat, in Asia and elsewhere, both to the sovereignty of the nation-state, and to the viability of some local cultures. But this does not necessarily mean an inevitable homogenising of all cultures. On the contrary, as the authority of the sovereign state is diminished, this may allow 'local cultures' that have been buried by the state, or other agencies, to emerge. Crisis, of one sort or another, is likely to hit many states in Asia, which need to commit themselves, to some extent, to the global economy in order to reap the benefits it can provide (investment, access to markets, technology), but at the same time are faced with the loss of control (economic, social and cultural) that goes with the concomitant 'liberalisation' of the civic, political and cultural spheres of the state. This process can be read, on the one hand, as an opportunity for marginalised and repressed groups to gain some level of political autonomy, and for the development of an educated and liberalised 'public sphere' free of state control or manipulation. On the other hand, global economics and inform- ationalism can be read as the reimposition by 'other means' of western hegemony (economic, political and cultural) in the Asia–Pacific region. Globalisation is likely to pave the way for a new kind of cultural 'imagining' which, although producing something far less durable than the habitus of the past, is potentially far more flexible, reflecting, if you like, the ability of cultural identities to adapt and change.

SUGGESTIONS FOR FURTHER READING

Chow, Rey (1993) *Writing Diaspora: Tactics of Intervention in Contemporary Cultural Studies*, Indiana University Press, Bloomington

Eickelman, Dale F. and J. W. Anderson (eds) (1999) *New Media in the Muslim World*, Indiana University Press, Bloomington

Fitzgerald, Stephen (1997) *Is Australia an Asian Country?* Allen & Unwin, Sydney

McGrew, Anthony and Christopher Brook (eds) (1998) *Asia-*

Pacific in the New World Order, Routledge, London and New York

Wilson, Rob and Arif Dirlik (eds) (1995) *Asia/Pacific as Space of Cultural Production*, Duke University Press, Durham and London

Glossary

Asian economic crisis   The so-called 'Asian economic crisis' can be traced back to early 1997, when South Korean and Thai businesses defaulted on their foreign debts. The 'contagion' quickly spread to other Asian countries such as Indonesia, Malaysia and even Japan. A number of reasons were put forward to explain how and why a group of countries which had, over a period of 30 years, experienced the highest levels of continuous growth in history should suddenly experience economic collapse. The most prevalent explanations were of the 'bubble effect' variety—Asian economies were overheated, stocks, realty and currencies were overvalued, and most of the affected countries had sizeable current account deficits (in contrast with countries such as Singapore, China and Taiwan, which had considerable surpluses, and avoided 'contamination'). The reason for this 'overheating' was tied up with the integration of those countries into the global economy, firstly as recipients of huge amounts of short-term investment attracted by their growth and high stock and realty values, and secondly because of the high level of exposure of countries such as Japan to these 'failed' economies (by way of loans, investment, markets). Once businesses defaulted or failed in Thailand and South Korea, international investment was quickly withdrawn, further accentuating the crisis. By 1999 the worst effects of the crisis had passed.

Asian 'tiger' economies   The collective name given to the great 'Asian economic success stories' (aside from Japan) of the last three decades—Singapore, Taiwan, South Korea and Hong Kong.

Asian values   The idea that there are ways of doing things, ideas, forms of governmentality, values and traditions that are specific to, and shared by, cultures and nations in Asia.

Colonialism   Colonialism usually refers to the overt violence and domination exercised by a more powerful counry over another. In the nineteenth century groups of people in Africa, Asia and other non-European areas were attacked by armies and navies, overwhelmed by superior military and other technologies, and enslaved or kept under political control (examples include the British Raj in India and Dutch rule in Indonesia). This violence was usually 'rationalised' through the argument that supposedly civilised countries (from the West) had a duty to 'improve' and educate 'barbaric' or 'backward' peoples (referred to as the 'white man's burden').

Communitarian values   The term communitarian values refers to valuing the welfare of the community over the 'freedom' of the individual.

Cultural flows   Cultural flows refers to the way in which electronic technology is able to disseminate cultural texts— films, television shows, sporting events, cartoons, music, pornographic images and stories, advertising, newspapers, magazines—across national borders.

Cultural literacy   Cultural literacy can be defined as 'both a knowledge of meaning systems and an ability to negotiate those systems within different cultural contexts' (Schirato & Yell, 1996/2000: 1).

Culture   Culture refers to texts of any kind which are used, generally, to produce meanings and, more specifically, in Arjun Appadurai's terms, to 'express, or set the groundwork for, the mobilization of group identities' (Appadurai, 1997: 13).

Deterritorialisation   Deterritorialisation refers to the way in which the attachment between communities and places is becoming less secure and certain. Local places are being 're-made' by global forces, which are forcing people to shift places. The flow of capital into different areas, or the decision of corporations to target or bypass locations with regard to the so-called information superhighway, can create localised economic booms or depressions almost overnight. Populations are responding to these developments by becoming extremely mobile, and are moving to areas (both inside and outside national borders) where work can be found. There are also the pressures and tensions associated with ethnic and religious separatism, which can make life extremely difficult and danger-ous for large diasporic communities.

Developmental strategies Developmental strategies refers to the attempts by so-called 'underdeveloped' countries to 'catch up' to the economies of the West. The great 'Asian economic success stories' of the last three decades (Japan and the so-called 'Asian tigers—Singapore, Taiwan, South Korea and Hong Kong), as well as some of the more 'developed' Asian economies (Thailand, Indonesia, Malaysia, Vietnam) have all, to some extent, based their economic policies on 'developmen-tal strategies' such as strong government intervention in the economy in the form of loans, subsidies, and policies which help foster growth. But there were other critical factors, including the maintenance of political 'stability' and continuity, industrial 'peace' (which kept labour costs down), and the protection of national markets from external competition (which allowed countries such as Japan, and later South Korea, to achieve considerable trade surpluses with the US and Europe). These conditions were achieved in different ways in different countries (contrast, for example, the 'business/labour accord' in Japan with the brutal repression of unions in Taiwan and South Korea).

Diasporas Diasporas can be defined as the dispersal and relocation of large groups of peoples sharing and further creating a common identity based on such things as race, ethnicity or nationality.

Endo-colonialism Endo-colonialism refers to the ways in which powerful national institutions (government, the army, businesses, bureaucracies) practise overt and covert forms of 'colonialist violence' against groups within their country through the use of physical violence and/or by denying them political rights (South Africa under 'apartheid' is an obvious example).

Enlightenment see **Modernity**

Ethnicity   The idea of ethnicity has usually been defined in terms of three main characteristics. Firstly, ethnic identities have been understood as relatively small, natural communities that predate nation-states. Secondly, ethnic identity is supposedly based on a shared culture and experiences (language, space, history, rituals, dress, food). And thirdly, ethnicity is understood as being based on what we could call 'blood-ties'—that is, biological similarities, kinship and skin colour.

Arjun Appadurai refers to this as the 'primordial' thesis of ethnicity. In its place, Appadurai has argued for what he calls a culturalist version of ethnicity. He points out that ethnic identities are no more 'natural' than nations. He accepts the primordialist assertion that ethnic groups are characterised by certain things that are shared (language, history, food, rituals, dress), but to this he adds the important point that these 'markers of group identity' have to be mobilised through the creation of a consciousness that values these markers, and the accompanying (ethnic) identity.

Gender   Gender refers to the notion that 'masculinity' and 'femininity' (and the values they come to represent) are always being 'renegotiated' as circumstances change. What is understood by the terms 'man' and 'woman' is in no way universal or ahistorical, but changes depending on cultural and historical circumstances, ideas and values.

Global capital   Global capital 'never stops working'—whether in stock markets, investment funds or banks. Huge amounts of capital are invested, relocated, accumulated, devalued, lost or withdrawn across the world every few seconds, which can have a serious, and sometimes catastrophic, effect on corporations, markets, regions, nations and the global economy itself.

Globalisation   Globalisation is usually understood as the way in which electronic technology—computer networks, satellites, fibre-optic cables—reduces the time it takes to send information, messages and images from one location to another, so that differences in space (countries, continents) become less relevant. But there is a lot more to globalisation than just overcoming long distances to do business.

Globalisation also refers to a specifically cultural phenomenon, that is, the way in which that same electronic technology is able to disseminate cultural texts—films, television shows, sporting events, cartoons, music, pornographic images and stories, advertising, newspapers, magazines—across national borders.

Habitus   Habitus is a term associated with the work of the French sociologist Pierre Bourdieu. It can be understood as a set of values, dispositions and practices which are behind just about everything we do and think, but which we have naturalised, and made unconscious.

Bourdieu argues that people's activities and behaviour are shaped by their cultural 'trajectories' (their parents, the schooling they received, religious institutions they were involved with, whether they came from working- or middle-class backgrounds), and the various 'fields of activity' they work in or come into contact with. Bourdieu suggests that every institution or field has its own authorised language (what Michel Foucault calls 'discourse'), as well as specific values, ways of doing things, expectations, hierarchies, dress codes and meanings. In order for a person to 'fit in' and progress (for instance, be employed and promoted in a business or bureaucracy) people are required to more or less 'unconsciously' adjust themselves to the institution or field they are in.

Imagined communities   Benedict Anderson argues that nation-states are really 'imagined communities'; that is, populations who come to believe and act as if they constitute a single, natural and more or less homogeneous entity. We can say that the different states of Asia, even the most supposedly 'natural' and traditional ones such as China and Japan, have been 'culturally imagined' into existence.

Informationalism   Informationalism can be understood in terms of changes in communication technology which have placed information, and its production, circulation, identification, retrieval and application at the centre of contemporary economic activity. This change has a profound effect on the field of economics and finance, producing a global economic system which has redefined what we understand by labour and capital, financial processes, the extent of government control of currency rates and other local economic factors, and the very idea of capitalism itself.

Liberalism   French theorist Michel Foucault argues that liberalism developed as a response to the strongly interventionist policies developed in the German states in the eighteenth century. Liberalism ushered in a significant change of direction for governmentality because it broke with the 'reason of state' which had emphasised interventionist policies aimed at ensuring the security and prosperity of the state. For liberalism, the state was a necessary evil—which might not even be necessary. Liberalism took advantage of the growing importance of economics to the state, and of the state's inclination to 'draw back' from intervening, in order to ensure the 'free enterprise of individuals'. Out of this process there develops a notion of 'civil society' as something more or less opposed to, critical of, or a check upon, governmentality.

Modernity   Modernity is usually understood as both a set of ideas or values closely tied to the Enlightenment, and as a set of institutions, technologies, practices and politics. The Enlightenment was the period of western history (the eighteenth century) characterised by a number of developments, including: the partial replacement of religion by 'human' values (liberty, equality, fraternity, individualism); the rise of science and scientific methods; a belief in reason, rationality and the civilising effects of culture and technology; and, a belief in 'progress'.

These beliefs and values gave rise to new institutions and practices—forms of democracy, educational institutions, political parties and movements, nation-states—which were exported, in time, to all parts of the globe. The extent to which a people could be designated—by the West—as civilised came to depend on whether or not they subscribed to, and developed, the beliefs, values, practices and institutions of 'enlightened' modernity.

Orientalism   Edward Said's book *Orientalism* (1978) puts forward the argument that the many different kinds of representations (books, policy documents, films, operas, television shows, paintings, photographs, media reports) of the Orient (loosely understood to include Asia and so-called 'Middle Eastern' countries) by the West are tied in with colonialist politics. In other words, there is no essential distinction between supposedly 'neutral' and apolitical cultural texts which deal with the orient and orientals and obvious anti-oriental political practices.

Postcolonialism   The twentieth century saw the development of covert forms of 'colonial' violence and domination, firstly through the continued influence, in previously colonised countries, of the 'overlay' of colonialism (institutions, language, political systems), and more insidiously through transnational and multinational corporations, world financial organisations such as the World Bank and the International Monetary Fund, and through the widespread dissemination of western culture. Although the age of colonisation has been replaced by what has been called 'postcolonialism', that 'post' refers not to an absence of colonising practices, but to their transformation and continuation through processes such as globalisation.

Postmodernity   Postmodernity, like modernity, can be understood both as a set of ideas or attitudes (postmodernism), and a specific historical period with its own technological developments, cultural styles and political practices. Postmodernity and its various characteristics are related to modernity as a development and enhancement, through the use of more powerful and efficient technologies, more sophisticated and widespread forms of capitalism, the shrinkage of space/time, an increase in the electronic media, communication networks, and images and discourses; and a reaction against its main principles, tenets and 'grand narratives' (such as the notion that developments in technology and science were necessarily progressive and universally beneficial).

Public sphere   Traditionally in the West the public sphere corresponded to a specific site or meeting place (a public square, for instance), where citizens could gather to discuss and debate their relation with the state and government. The public sphere was considered essential because it was meant to help citizens learn, and make informed decisions, about their society. With modern states it became impossible to gather citizens together in one place—although certain places are still used by the people when they want to protest against their governments. In the contemporary world the media has become the site that links the public. This role of substitute 'public sphere' has largely been seen, in the West, to have been taken on by non-commercial and non-aligned institutions such as the UK public broadcaster the BBC, but increasingly it has come to include all the media, especially the Internet.

Bibliography

Anderson, Benedict (1991) *Imagined Communities: Reflections on the Origin and Spread of Nationalism*, rev. edn, Verso, London

Anwar, Ibrahim (1996) *The Asian Renaissance*, Times Books International, Singapore and Kuala Lumpur

Appadurai, Arjun (1990) 'Disjuncture and difference in the global cultural economy', *Public Culture* 2, 1–24

—(1997) *Modernity at Large*, University of Minnesota Press, Minneapolis

Ashcroft, Bill, Gareth Griffiths and Helen Tiffin (1998) *Key Concepts in Post-Colonial Studies*, Routledge, London and New York

Asiaweek, 7 August 1998

Balibar, Etienne and Immanuel Wallerstein (1991) *Race, Nation, Class: Ambiguous Identities*, Verso, New York

Baudrillard, J. (1993) *Symbolic Exchange and Death*, trans. I. Grant, Sage, London

Bell, Roger, Tim McDonald and Alan Tidwell (eds) (1996) *Negotiating the Pacific Century: The 'New' Asia, The United States and Australia*, Allen & Unwin, Sydney

Bersani, Leo (1986) *The Freudian Body: Psychoanalysis and Art*, Columbia University Press, New York

Bhabha, Homi K. (ed.) (1990) *Nation and Narration*, Routledge, London and New York

—(1994) *The Location of Culture*, Routledge, London and New York

Birch, David (ed.) (1995) *Framing (Post-Colonial) Cultures*, a special issue of *Southern Review* 28:3

—(1996) 'Constructing identities and "responsible" citizens: Australia, Korea and some issues of cultural theory', *Australian Studies* 3:1, 3–20

—(1998a) 'An "open" environment? Asian case studies and the regulation of public culture', *Continuum: Journal of Media and Cultural Studies* 12:3, 335–48

—(1998b) 'Communication policy in Asia: limited democracy and the public sphere', *Media International Australia: Culture and Policy* 86, 87–102

—(1998c) 'Public cultures: "Asian" and "Australian" spaces', *Southern Review* 64–73

—(ed.) (1998d) *Asian Values: Public Cultures*, a special double issue of *Social Semiotics* 8:2/3

Bourdieu, P. (1991) *Outline of a Theory of Practice*, trans. R. Nice, Cambridge University Press, Cambridge

Buchanan, Ian (ed.) (1997) *A Deleuzian Century?*, a special issue of *The South Atlantic Quarterly* 96:3

Butler, Judith (1990) *Gender Trouble: Feminism and the Subversion of Identity* Routledge, New York and London

Castells, Manuel (1993) *The Informational City*, Blackwell, Oxford

—(1997a) *The Power of Identity*, vol. 2 in his *The Information Age: Economy, Society and Culture*, Blackwell, Oxford

—(1997b) *The Rise of the Network Society*, Blackwell, Oxford

—(1998) *End of Millennium*, Blackwell, Oxford

Chan, Heng Chee (ed.) (1997) *The New Asia-Pacific Order*, Institute of Southeast Asian Studies, Singapore

Chatterjee, P. (1993) *The Nation and Its Fragments*, Colonial and Postcolonial Histories, Princeton University Press, Princeton

Chen, Kuan-Hsing (ed.) (1998) *Trajectories: Inter-Asia Cultural Studies*, in the series *Culture and Communication in Asia*, general editor David Birch, Routledge, London

Chow, Rey (1991) *Woman and Chinese Modernity: The Politics of Reading Between West and East*, University of Minnesota Press, Minneapolis

—(1993a) 'Listening other wise: music miniaturized; a different type of question about revolution', in S. During (ed.) (1993) *The Cultural Studies Reader*, Routledge, London

—(1993b) *Writing Diaspora: Tactics of Intervention in Contemporary Cultural Studies*, Indiana University Press, Bloomington

—(1998) *Ethics after Idealism: Theory, Culture, Ethnicity, Reading*, Indiana University Press, Bloomington

Chua, Beng Huat (1995) *Communitarian Ideology and Democracy in Singapore*, Routledge, London and New York

Clifford, J. (1988) *The Predicament of Culture*, Harvard University Press, Cambridge, Mass.

Connell, R.W. (1995) *Masculinities*, Allen & Unwin, Sydney

Constantino, Renato (1998) 'Globalization and the south: the Philippines experience', in Kuan-Hsing Chen (ed.) (1998) *Trajectories: Inter-Asia Cultural Studies*, Routledge, London

Coté, J. (1992) *Letters from Kartini*, Monash University, Melbourne

Danaher, Geoff, Tony Schirato and Jen Webb (2000) *Understanding Foucault*, Allen & Unwin, Sydney

Darby, Phillip (ed.) (1997) *At the Edge of International Relations: Postcolonialism, Gender and Dependency*, Pinter, London and New York

Das, Veena (1996) *Critical Events: An Anthropological Perspective on Contemporary India*, Oxford University Press, Perth

Dean, Kenneth (1998) 'Despotic empire/nation-state: local responses to Chinese nationalism in an age of global capitalism', in Kuan-Hsing Chen (ed.) (1998) *Trajectories: Inter-Asia Cultural Studies*, Routledge, London

Dirlik, Arif (1994) *After the Revolution: Waking to Global Capitalism*, Wesleyan University Press, Hanover

Dobbs-Higginson, M.S. (1993) *Asia Pacific: Its Role in the New World Disorder*, Longman, London

Docherty, Thomas (ed.) (1993) *Postmodernism: A Reader*, Harvester Wheatsheaf, New York

Drèze, J. and J. Loh (1995) 'Literacy in India and China', in *Economic and Political Weekly*, vol. xxx, no. 45: 2868–78

Drucker, Peter F. (1993) *Post Capitalist Society*, HarperCollins, New York

Duara, Praesenjit (1995) *Rescuing History From the Nation: Questioning Narratives of Modern China*, The University of Chicago Press, Chicago

Eickelman, Dale F. and J.W. Anderson (eds) (1999) *New Media in the Muslim World*, Indiana University Press, Bloomington

Featherstone, Mike (ed.) (1990) *Global Culture: Nationalism, Globalization and Modernity*, Sage, London

—, S. Lash and R. Robertson (eds) (1995) *Global Modernities*, Sage, London

Ferguson, Russel, Martha Gever, Trinh T. Minh-ha and Cornel West (eds) (1990) *Out There: Marginalization and Contemporary Cultures*, MIT Press, Cambridge, Mass.

Ferro, M. (1997) *Colonization: A Global History*, Routledge, London and New York

Fitzgerald, Stephen (1997) *Is Australia an Asian Country?* Allen & Unwin, Sydney

Foucault, M. (1997) *Ethics: The Essential Works 1*, editor P. Rabinow, trans. R. Hurley, Penguin, London

Frankel, B. (1983) *Beyond the State? Dominant Theories and Socialist Strategies*, Macmillan, London

Fukuyama, Francis (1995) *Trust: The Social Virtues and the Creation of Prosperity*, The Free Press, New York

Ghandi, Leela (1998) *Postcolonial Theory*, Allen & Unwin, Sydney; Columbia University Press, New York; Edinburgh University Press, Edinburgh

Garnaut, Ross and Peter Drysdale (eds) with John Kunkel (1994) *Asia Pacific Regionalism: Readings in International Economic Relations*, Harper Educational, Sydney

Gay, P. (1973) *The Enlightenment: An Interpretation*, Wildwood House, London

Giddens, Anthony (1990) *The Consequences of Modernity*, Polity Press, Cambridge

—(1991) *Modernity and Self-identity: Self and Society in the Late Modern Age*, Polity Press, Cambridge

Grewal, Inderpal and Caren Kaplan (eds) (1994) *Scattered Hegemonies: Postmodernity and Transnational Feminist Practices*, University of Minnesota Press, Minneapolis

Habermas, Jurgen (1989) *The Stuctural Transformation of the Public Sphere: An Inquiry into a Category of Bourgeois Society*, MIT Press, Cambridge, Mass.

Hall, Stuart (ed.) (1997) *Representation: Cultural Representation and Signifying Practices*, Sage, London, in the *Culture, Media and Identities* series

— and Paul du Gay (eds) (1996) *Questions of Cultural Identity*, Sage, London

— and Don Hubert (eds) (1996) *Modernity: An Introduction to Modern Societies*, Blackwell, Oxford

Hannerz, U. (1996) *Transnational Connections, Culture, People, Places*, Routledge, London and New York

Harlow, Barbara and Mia Carter (eds) (1999) *Imperialism and Orientalism: A Documentary Sourcebook*, Blackwell, Oxford

Hasan, M. (ed.) (1998) *Islam, Communities and the Nation: Muslim Identities in South Asia and Beyond*, Manohar, New Delhi

Hill, Michael and Lan Kwen Fee (1995) *The Politics of Nation Building and Citizenship in Singapore*, Routledge, London and New York

Hobart, Mark (ed.) (1995) *An Anthropological Critique of Development: The Growth of Ignorance*, Routledge, London and New York

Hooper, B. (1998) 'Flower vase and housewife: women and consumerism in post-Mao China', in K. Sen and M. Stivens (eds) *Gender and Power in Affluent Asia*, Routledge, London and New York, pp. 167–93

Huntington, Samuel. P. (1997) *The Clash of Civilizations and the Remaking of the World Order*, Simon & Schuster, London

Jahan, R. (1992) *Women in Asia*, Minority Rights Group, London

Jain, D., M. Singh and M. Chand (1992) 'India', in R. Jahan (ed.) *Women in Asia*, Minority Rights Group, London

Jayawardena, K. (1992) 'Sri Lanka' in R. Jahan (ed.) *Women in Asia*, Minority Rights Group, London

Jeffrey, R. (1992) *Politics, Women and Well Being: How Kerala Became a 'Model'*, Macmillan Press, Basingstoke

Jones, Dylan (2000) 'Are men the new women?', *Independent International*, 23–29 February: 20

Kabbani, Rana (1986) *Europe's Myths of the Orient*, Pandora Press, London

Kahn, Joel (1995) *Culture, Multiculture, Postculture*, Sage, London

Kakar, S. (1990) *Intimate Relations: Exploring Indian Sexuality*, University of Chicago Press, Chicago

Kelly, David and Anthony Reid (eds) (1998) *Asian Freedoms: The Idea of Freedom in East and Southeast Asia*, Cambridge University Press, Cambridge

Kumar, R. (1993) *The History of Doing. An Illustrated Account of Movement for Women's Rights and Feminism in India*, Kali for Women, New Delhi

Laothamatas, Anek (ed.) (1997) *Democratization in Southeast and East Asia*, Institute of Southeast Asian Studies, Singapore

Lash, Scott (1999) *Another Modenity: A Different Rationality*, Blackwell, Oxford

Leonard, P. and K. Harrison (1997) 'Satellite broadcasting: the Asia market', paper presented to the International Bar Association Conference, Delhi, November 2–7

Lim, Shirley Geok-Lin, Larry E. Smith and Wimal Dissanayake (eds) (1999) *Transnational Asia Pacific: Gender, Culture and the Public Sphere*, University of Illinois Press, Champaign

Lowe, Lisa (1991) *Critical Terrains: French and British Orientalisms*, Cornell University Press, Ithaca

— and David Lloyd (eds) (1997) *The Politics of Culture in the Shadow of Capital*, in the series *Post-Contemporary Interventions*, general editors Stanley Fish and Frederic Jameson, Duke University Press, Durham and London

McGrew, Anthony and Christopher Brook (eds) (1998) *Asia-Pacific in the New World Order*, Routledge, London and New York

McLaren, A.E. (1998) 'Chinese cultural revivalism: changing gender constructions in the Yangtze River Delta', in K. Sen and M. Stivens (eds) *Gender and Power in Affluent Asia*, Routledge, London and New York, pp. 195–221

Madan, T.N. (ed.) (1995) *Muslim Communities of South Asia: Culture, Society and Power*, Manohar, New Delhi

Matsui, Y. (1999) *Women in the New Asia*, Zed Books, London and New York

Mattelart, Armand (1994) *Mapping World Communication: War, Progress, Culture* trans. Susan Emmanuel and James A. Cohen, University of Minnesota Press, Minneapolis

—(1996) *The Invention of Communication*, trans. Susan Emmanuel, University of Minnesota Press, Minneapolis

Milner, Anthony and Mary Quilty (eds) (1996) *Australia in Asia: Comparing Cultures*, Oxford University Press, Melbourne

Mohanty, Chandra, Ann Russo and Lourdes Torres (1991) *Third World Women and the Politics of Feminism*, Indiana University Press, Bloomington

Montes, Manuel F. and Vladimir V. Popov (1999) *The Asian Crisis Turns Global*, Institute of Southeast Asian Studies, Singapore

Morley, David and Kuan-Hsing Chen (eds) (1996) *Stuart Hall: Critical Dialogues in Cultural Studies*, Routledge, London and New York

Morley, David and Kevin Robins (1995) *Spaces of Identity: Global Media, Electronic Landscapes and Cultural Boundaries*, Routledge, London and New York

Muzaffar, C. (1988) 'Islamic resurgence: a global view', in T. Abdullah and S. Siddique (eds) (1988) *Islam and Society in Southeast Asia*, Institute of Southeast Asian Studies, Singapore

Neher, Clark D. (1991) *Southeast Asia in the New International Era*, Westview Press, Boulder

Ng, King Kang (1999) *The Rainbow Connection: The Internet and the Singapore Gay Community*, KangCuBine Publishing, Singapore

Nguyen-vo, Thu-Luong (1997) 'Prostitution in a liberalizing Vietnam: The economy, hierarchy and geography of pleasure', paper prepared for the ASPAC conference at Asiloma, June 26–29

Ohmae, Kenichi (1991) *The Borderless World: Power and Strategy in the Interlinked Economy*, Harper Business, New York, rev. edn, 1999

—(1995) *The End of the Nation State: The Rise of Regional Economies*, HarperCollins, London

Pandey, G. (1994) *The Construction of Communism in Colonial North India*, Oxford University Press, Delhi

Pateman, Carole (1988) *The Sexual Contract*, Blackwell, Oxford

Perera, Suvendrini (ed.) (1995) *Asia and Pacific Inscriptions: Identities, Ethnicities, Nationalities*, Meridian, Melbourne

Preston, Peter (1998) *Pacific Asia in the Global System: An Introduction*, Blackwell, Oxford

Robison, Richard (ed.) (1996) *Pathways to Asia: The Politics of Engagement*, Allen & Unwin, Sydney

Ronan, Colin and Joseph Needham (1980) *The Shorter Science and Civilisation in China*, vol. 1, Cambridge University Press, Cambridge

Rowen, Henry S. (ed.) (1998) *Behind East Asian Growth: The Political and Social Foundations of Prosperity*, Routledge, London and New York

Said, Edward (1978) *Orientalism: Western Conceptions of the Orient*, Routledge, London and New York, 2nd edn published in 1985

Sardar, Ziauddin (1998) *Postmodernism and the Other: The New Imperialism of Western Culture*, Pluto Press, London

Schirato, Tony and Susan Yell (1996) *Communication and Cultural Literacy: An Introduction,* 2nd edition 2000, Allen & Unwin, Sydney; Sage, London

Schwartz, Peter and Blair Gibb (1999) *When Good Companies Do Bad Things: Responsibility and Risk in an Age of Globalisation,* John Wiley & Sons, New York

Scott, Alan (ed.) (1997) *The Limits of Globalization: Cases and Arguments,* Routledge, London and New York

Sen, Krishna and M. Stivens (eds) *Gender and Power in Affluent Asia,* Routledge, London and New York

Shahar, M. and R.P. Weller (eds) (1996) *Unruly Gods: Divinity and Society in China,* University of Hawaii Press, Honolulu

Sinha, M. (1997) *Colonial Masculinity. The 'Manly Englishman' and the 'Effeminate Bengali' in the Nineteenth Century,* Kali for Women, New Delhi

Smith, Patrick (1997) 'What East Asia really needs is more democracy', editorial in the *International Herald,* 11 December: 8

Spivak, G.C. (1987) *In Other Worlds: Essays in Cultural Politics,* Methuen, New York

Srinivas, M.N. (1962) *Caste in Modern India and Other Essays,* Asia, Bombay

Srivastava, Sanjay (1998) *Constructing Post-Colonial India: National Character and the Doon School,* in the series *Culture and Communication in Asia,* general editor David Birch, Routledge, London

Stivens, M. (1996) *Matriliny and Modernity. Sexual Politics and Social Change in Rural Malaysia,* Allen & Unwin, Sydney

Tanaka, Stefan (1993) *Japan's Orient: Rendering Pasts into History,* University of California Press, Berkeley

Thompson, L.G. (1975) *Chinese Religion: An Introduction,* Dickenson Publishing Company, Encino and Belmont, California

Thurow, Lester (1996) *The Future of Capitalism,* Penguin, New York

Tomlinson, John (1999) *Globalization and Culture,* Polity Press, Cambridge

Trinh T. Minh-ha (1989) *Woman, Native, Other: Writing, Postcoloniality and Feminism,* Indiana University Press, Bloomington

Turner, Bryan S. (1994) *Orientalism, Postmodernism and Globalism,* Routledge, London and New York

— (ed.) (1990) *Theories of Modernity and Postmodernity*, Sage, London

Uberoi, Patricia (1998) *Social Reform, Sexuality and the State,* in the *Contributions to Indian Sociology* occasional series no 7, Sage, London

Vatikiotis, Michael R.J. (1996) *Political Change in Southeast Asia. Trimming the Banyan Tree*, Routledge, London

Viswanathan, G. (1989) *Masks of Conquest: Literary Study and British Rule in India*, Columbia University Press, New York

Vitebsky, Piers (1995) *The Shaman*, Little Brown Co, New York

Werbner, P. (1995) 'The ranking of brotherhoods: the dialectics of Muslim caste among overseas Pakistanis', in T.N. Madan (ed.) (1995) *Muslim Communities of South Asia: Culture, Society and Power*, Manohar, New Delhi

Williams, Patrick and Laura Chrisman (eds) (1994) *Colonial Discourse and Post-Colonial Theory: A Reader*, Columbia University Press, New York

Wilson, Rob and Arif Dirlik (eds) (1995) *Asia/Pacific as Space of Cultural Production*, Duke University Press, Durham and London

Wilson, Rob and Wimal Dissanayake (eds) (1996) *Global/Local: Cultural Production and the Transnational Imaginary*, in the series *Asia-Pacific Culture, Politics and Society*, general editors Rey Chow, H.D. Harootunian and Masao Miyoshi, Duke University Press, Durham and London

Wink, A. (1987) 'The Jewish diaspora in India: eighth to thirteenth centuries' *Indian Economic and Social History Review*, 24, 4:349–66

Wodak, Ruth, Rudolf de Cillia, Martin Reisigl and Karen Liebhart (1999) *The Discursive Construction of National Identity*, trans. Angelika Hirsch and Richard Mitten, Edinburgh University Press, Edinburgh

Wu, D.Y.H., H. McQueen and Y. Yamamoto (eds) (1997) *Emerging Pluralism in Asia and the Pacific*, Hong Kong Institute of Asia Pacific Studies, Hong Kong

Yamamoto, Tadashi (ed.) (1995) *Emerging Civil Society in the Asia Pacific Community*, Institute of Southeast Asian Studies, Singapore

Yao, Souchou (1994) 'The predicament of modernity: mass media and the making of the west in Southeast Asia', *Asian Journal of Communication* 4:1, 33–51

Yeo, George (1994) 'The technological revolution poses threats or opportunities', *Media Asia*, 21(2):104–6

Zutshi, S. (1993) 'Women, nation and the outsider in contemporary Hindi cinema', in T. Niranjana, P. Sudhira and V. Dhareshwar (eds) *Interrogating Modernity–Culture and Colonialism in India*, Seagull, Calcutta

Index

211

ASIA